The

SH!T

No One Tells You About

DIVORCE

ALSO BY DAWN DAIS

The Sh!t No One Tells You:
A Guide to Surviving Your Baby's First Year

The Sh!t No One Tells You About Pregnancy:
A Guide to Surviving Pregnancy, Childbirth, and Beyond

The Sh!t No One Tells You About Baby #2:
A Guide to Surviving Your Growing Family

The Sh!t No One Tells You About Toddlers:
A Guide to Surviving the Toddler Years

The Nonrunner's Marathon Guide for Women:
Get Off Your Butt and On with Your Training

The Noncyclist's Guide to the Century
and Other Road Races: Get on Your Butt and Into Gear

The
SH!T
No One Tells You About
DIVORCE

A GUIDE TO BREAKING UP, FALLING APART, AND PUTTING YOURSELF BACK TOGETHER

Dawn Dais

hachette
BOOKS
NEW YORK

Hachette Go, an imprint of Hachette Books
Hachette Book Group
1290 Avenue of the Americas
New York, NY 10104
HachetteGo.com
Facebook.com/HachetteGo
Instagram.com/HachetteGo

First Edition: January 2023

Hachette Books is a division of Hachette Book Group, Inc.

The Hachette Go and Hachette Books name and logos are trademarks of Hachette Book Group, Inc.

The publisher is not responsible for websites (or their content) that are not owned by the publisher.

Print book interior design by Jeff Williams.

Library of Congress Cataloging-in-Publication Data
Names: Dais, Dawn, author.
Title: The sh!t no one tells you about divorce : a guide to breaking up, falling apart, and putting yourself back together / Dawn Dais.
Description: First edition. | New York : Hachette Go, 2023.
Identifiers: LCCN 2022042422 | ISBN 9780306828546 (paperback) | ISBN 9780306828553 (ebook)
Subjects: LCSH: Divorce. | Self-actualization (Psychology)
Classification: LCC HQ814 .D29 2023 | DDC 306.89—dc23/eng/20220922
LC record available at https://lccn.loc.gov/2022042422

ISBNs: 978-0-306-82854-6 (trade paperback); 978-0-306-82855-3 (ebook)

Printed in the United States of America

LSC-C

Printing 1, 2022

We don't talk about grief as a part of change enough. . . . [I]t does people a disservice. Because when they hit grief, they think they've done something wrong. . . . Change always includes a series of small deaths. And if we don't understand that grief is going to be a part of change and that loss is going to be a part of change, I don't think we can successfully evolve.

—BRENÉ BROWN

So where do we find grace and light? If you mean right now, the answer is Nowhere. . . . Grace always does bat last, and the light always overcomes the darkness—always, historically. But not necessarily later the same day, or tomorrow, after lunch.

—ANNE LAMOTT

When you are going through a hard time just eat ice cream in a dark place. Get a bunch of different flavors.

—MY DAUGHTER'S 10-YEAR-OLD FRIEND

Do you know why divorces are so expensive? Because they are worth it.

—WILLIE NELSON

Contents

Introduction

Welcome to Your Meantime

In the beginning of my divorce, when everything had gone ass over teakettle and life felt very, very raw, my divorced friends would repeatedly assure me that everything would be okay. They were a few years ahead of me on their divorce timelines, and they knew from experience that things would eventually calm down. They'd tell me, "Just give it time, everything will be fine, you guys will be fine. Just give it time."

I'd respond with, "Yeah, that's great. But what the hell am I supposed to do in the meantime?"

The "meantime" of divorce is brutal. It's the time between the end of your marriage and the beginning of feeling normal in the new version of your life. The meantime is the time required for that new version of life to feel worn in instead of ill-fittingly new.

The good news is, my friends were right, time did help, and everything did end up settling down into a comfortable new normal. The bad news is, there are no shortcuts through the meantime.

Trust me on that one, because I repeatedly tried (and failed) to speed up my meantime. I tried to MacGyver the broken parts back together, I tried just blaming everything on my ex, I tried putting my fingers in my ears, closing my eyes, and yelling, "Everything is FINE!" over and over again. You'll be shocked to learn that none of those strategies were successful.

I've written this book for those of you still working through your meantime. Because I know how confusing and isolating and infuriating that time can be. I know how aggressively odd it is to keep moving through all of life's responsibilities when your head and your heart and your entire friggin' world feel like a snow globe that has been shaken up by a three year old on a sugar high.

I wanted to write a book to remind you that you are not crazy, you are not irrevocably damaged, you are just a human navigating a ridiculously complicated period of your life. Also, as I mentioned previously, you have some time to kill, so why not flip through a profanity-laced book about divorce while you wait for your snow globe to pull its shit together?

The book you hold in your hands is a pretty detailed account of my meantime. It is messy and raw, introspective and evolved, and everything in between. At times my words are enlightened, self-centered, shattered, crazy, appalling, and kind. And that is just a sampling of the myriad of emotions that are constantly swirling around during the meantime. What an exciting life experience!

I tried to be as honest as possible in writing this book, while still being conscious of the fact that I am writing in permanent ink about quite a few other people whose lives were exploded along with mine. It was a delicate dance that I'm not sure I always pulled off, but I hope the end result is balanced and that our journey can provide a little camaraderie to others traveling a similar path.

In an effort to add to that camaraderie I chatted with a lot of other divorcées over the past couple of years. I refer to these men and women as my Divorce Squad throughout the book, and I've included their stories and opinions to expand upon mine. All their names have been changed, and I feel genuinely grateful that they all trusted me with their truth and vulnerability.

I would talk for hours with different members of my Divorce Squad, each of their stories varying wildly from each other and from my own. But no matter the details, there seemed to be a through line in all of our narratives, a universality to what it really feels like to have everything fall the fuck apart. There was an ease to our conversations because letting go of all pretense is pretty freeing when you've been pretending to hold it together for so long. Instead of the standard, "Yeah, everything is *totally* fine," these conversations started with, "It was not fine, and let me tell you all about it." From there, we were off and running.

These conversations inspired one of my favorite parts of this book. During each Divorce Squad chat, I would share that I was trying to get into the right headspace for writing, because I didn't think it would be appropriate to write an entire book with every chapter titled, "Fuck You, You Fucking Fuck."

All the divorced people would laugh at this joke. And then EVERY SINGLE ONE would say, "But I'd like to read *that* book."

It got me thinking.

Healing from divorce is a long process, and it's not necessarily a linear one. Some days are better than others, and sometimes your "namaste" efforts are no match for your "oh, for fuck's sake" reality. Often, just when you think you're making headway, something will throw you offtrack. Your ex will do something particularly ridiculous, or you'll come across a video on your phone of your life pre-split, or you'll be engulfed by the loneliness of your new reality.

On those days you might not be feeling particularly mature or evolved or healed. On those days you may just really want to scream, "Fuck you, you fucking FUCK!" And I'm in full support of such screaming. So much so that I decided to include regular rage journaling interludes throughout this book. The "Fuck You, You Fucking Fuck" journal prompts are scattered among the chapters as a place for you to let go of all pretense and lean into the things that are not fine. They are a safe place for your profanity to roam.

This book focuses heavily on divorce when kids are involved (our girl/boy were nine/seven years old when we split), because that was the particular shit show I had to navigate, but no matter what the circumstance of your split or where you are in your meantime, I hope this book can help you as you make your way to the other side.

Pull up a seat and let's commiserate for a little while. We'll rage and laugh and introspect and cry. And cuss. We are going to cuss a lot. There can be no healing without a fair amount of cussing, it's just science. You're welcome.

1

The Long Goodbye

(marriages break apart tiny pieces at a time)

My ex, Elizabeth, used to wash her hands several times a day, wipe them on a paper towel, then throw the paper towel on the counter, instead of throwing it away. Every day. Multiple paper towels, all over my counter, that I was left to clean up. This started to absolutely infuriate me; these paper towels caused a seething blind rage.

One time I conducted an experiment where, instead of throwing the paper towels away, I piled them up on the counter, creating a multimedia art installation of sorts. It could have been titled *Grown-Ass Woman Can't Throw Away Her Own Garbage*. Elizabeth shrugged off my art piece and even added to it herself, to demonstrate that I shouldn't be trying to teach her lessons like she was a child.

And that's the kind of moment you just know things are going smashingly well in a relationship.

•••

In a long partnership it's expected that things will ebb and flow with good times and bad. But when the flow of bad times starts to overpower the good times, it can inspire a bit of introspection. We take a hard look at what we've built and really consider whether it has any value left at all. When the answer is no, we often don't want to admit that we've invested so much into something that should be thrown in the trash pile. So, we hang on to it, we polish it up with some couple's therapy and date nights. Maybe take a weekend getaway to duct tape the broken parts.

We do this over and over again, sometimes throughout years and years, ignoring the cracks, pretending the glimmers of good are enough. Until finally something too big to ignore lands the finishing blow.

In chats with my Divorce Squad, I've found that a good deal of divorces come about after some sort of big, rattling event. Cheating is a common one. Mental illness. Egregious financial deceit. Often there's something significant that triggers the final time of death. But even in those cases, I tend to believe the relationship was most likely slowly breaking down well before the inciting incident.

When I asked my Divorce Squad about the moment they knew their marriages were over, most of them homed in on moments that occurred well before they actually got divorced. Because that's what relationships are, really, a series of moments, each of them moving us closer together or further apart.

In my case, the series of moments included a series of paper towels. The paper towels were indicative of other issues, obviously. With two small kids and a partner, I felt like my life had become consumed by caring for other people, and I was deeply resentful that Elizabeth seemed, in my mind, unwilling to do basic tasks to carry her weight. Basic tasks like throwing away a MOTHER-@#$@#$ paper towel.

Instead of addressing my paper towel rage or trying to get to the root of why a piece of garbage sent me over the edge, I simply pushed my feelings down and piled them on top of everything else I was barely holding together. Moment after moment, I pushed more and more down.

A huge part of my navigating to the other side of my divorce was the work I did to unpack the years I spent with my ex—and all the things besides the paper towels that I had pushed down for so long. I had to look at that time with honest eyes, own my part in it, and wrap my mind around the whys of it all. Why had I given up on us? Why did I stay for so long in such a bad relationship? Why did I become such an ugly version of myself for the person I'd chosen to do life with?

There's a popular metaphor about boiling frogs that I think applies to the souring of long-term relationships. The idea is that you can't throw a frog into boiling water, because the frog will jump out, knowing the temperature is too hot. But if you put a frog in lukewarm water and then gradually increase the temperature, the frog won't be aware that he is slowly being boiled. Relationships can be the same. (I know, I should write love poems for Hallmark cards.)

When you first get into the pot with your partner, things are comfortable, but then slowly life starts to boil a little bit at a time. Maybe you are trying to juggle career and parenthood, and you feel like your spouse isn't carrying their weight. Maybe you spend your days meeting everyone else's needs and never quite get around to that self-care you see all over social media. Maybe it's been months since you've slept with your partner, or even wanted them to touch you. Maybe the two of you took on too much debt and are struggling to get out from underneath it. Maybe you haven't had a proper night's sleep in years and are just. so. tired. Maybe you and your spouse stopped really seeing each other years ago. Maybe this just wasn't what you thought life would feel like.

Tick, tick, tick. The water gets more and more uncomfortable.

In my case we'd done a really good job building a really big life. Two kids, two thriving careers, five properties, and eight animals. But our life felt very heavy, and I felt like I was carrying too much of the load. So even little things—like paper towels strewn about the kitchen—seemed heavier than they actually were, simply because I was already maxed out.

I've heard it said that there are two types of relationships, compatible and complementary. Compatible couples tend to have more in common, whereas the complementary couples balance each other with their differences. Complementary couples can start off very strong, with that whole "opposites attract" thing working in their favor, but research shows that compatible couples have greater longevity.

In my independent studies I've found that the things you once framed as "complementary" can become "tedious as shit" as the years wear on and as your polar opposite partner wears on you.

Once Elizabeth and I had kids, it became much harder to ignore how differently we moved through the world. As our life started to feel heavier, I began to realize how much of the weight was from our relationship, and that's when things started breaking apart.

She operated at what I perceived as a heightened level of emotion at all times; every day she was spinning out about one thing or another. Once baby rearing came on the docket, I just no longer had the bandwidth to indulge the spins. So instead, I would completely disconnect, appearing numb and vacant most of the time. In truth, I was simply stuffing away any and all emotions, because I didn't feel like there was any space for them in her orbit. This made Elizabeth feel utterly alone in our relationship, because I was so detached and ice cold. As a result, she would spin more, trying to rattle me awake.

None of my ex's behaviors were malicious; they were just a result of how her brain is wired. And that wiring just happened to be very different from mine. But it's a weird thing being emptied out by a person who means well. And it was probably equally weird for her to watch her partner fall out of love with her for being who she'd been since Day 1.

The whole thing happened slowly, just like with that boiling frog. It was so slow that it was almost unnoticeable. And it included what could only be described as me gaslighting myself.

I'd rationalize, over and over again, "She's a good mom, we have a good life, she's a good, loyal person, she means well." Years and years of this, until eventually I could no longer talk myself out of our reality.

In thinking back to our breaking point, when I knew for sure there was no value left in this thing we'd built, there's one moment that stands out.

I've had bad hearing since I was a kid. My pregnancies exacerbated the hearing loss, to the point where I was completely deaf in one ear and barely getting by with a hearing aid in the other. At one not so fun appointment, my audiologist informed me that I was going deaf. It was only a matter of time before all of my limited hearing would be gone. I always knew this would happen eventually, but I somehow thought I had more time. I was only forty-one years old. Deaf.

After that appointment I sat in the parking lot, in my car, and cried. It was one of the saddest and scariest moments of my life. But I didn't call my partner. It was a couple weeks before I even told her the news.

If I told her I was going deaf, somehow the conversation would end with me having to calm her down, me having to manage her emotions about it. Our years together had shown me over and over again that there would not be room for all the swirling emotions I was having about going deaf.

If I hadn't known before, I knew for sure in that parking lot that Elizabeth was not the person I wanted to do life with anymore. In fact, it was clear that I had already stopped doing life with her, since it wasn't even an option to call her when I was crying in that car, in that parking lot, in one of the worst moments of my life. She was no longer my person.

When I think about it now, with clear eyes, I see that I didn't even give Elizabeth the chance to step up and support me the way I needed at that time. I had decided years prior who she was and who she could be, and in doing so had shut us both off to the possibility of being better for each other.

The point of this chapter, and these stories, isn't to put my ex on blast. I actually hesitated to even tell these parts of our story at all, because what's the point of rehashing old news? If I've moved on, why does any of this matter?

But the fact is, I wasn't able to really move on from my partnership until I realized how much our time together mattered. I couldn't really find my way back until I took a hard look at how far gone I had allowed myself to drift in our twelve years. Our story isn't particularly dramatic, and cleaning up paper towels is not exactly akin to surviving abuse or adultery. But I think a lot of marriages die in similar ways. In the tiny resentments and exhaustions that build and fester over years and years, until there is no value left at all.

The rest of this book is about taking stock of the destruction of divorce and figuring out how to put things back together in better ways. But in my case, I couldn't assemble anything new until I was honest about the decade of construction errors I'd made previously.

Marriages are long and complex and nuanced. Divorce is rarely a one-man job. A lot of the hurdles that came after our split tied directly to our years together. To our old habits, our worn-in assumptions, our defense mechanisms, and deep injuries.

In the beginning of our end, all of those things seemed nearly impossible to overcome. And maybe yours seem impossible too. But my ex and I made it to the other side of impossible. And I think you can too.

The long goodbye of a failed relationship doesn't end with a split or divorce. The process of actually getting to a place of *done* continues well after paperwork has been signed and household goods have been split up. Even if you feel done with the relationship, odds are it's not totally done with you just yet.

Getting to the end of your long goodbye is going to take some work. Start thinking about more than just the end of your relationship; rummage around in the other moments as well. Those times, both recent and ancient, big and small, when you started moving a little further away from your spouse.

It can be really hard to do this digging in the immediate aftermath of a divorce, especially if the end felt sudden or brutal. But when you are ready, these moments are going to be the key to not only understanding what went wrong in your past relationship but learning how you can do better in all parts of your life moving forward.

Because Lord knows we don't need to learn these lessons more than once.

••••

In the Meantime

My long goodbye extended for quite a while before I got to the point where I was ready to acknowledge my own role in my failed relationship. The acceptance and the moving on and all the other Zen shit were not part of my early divorce days. And I don't expect them to be a part of your early days either.

So, in the meantime, while Zen is not yet on your list of things to do, here are some other activities to pass the time.

Not Today, Zen

- Dance around your house, in your underwear, singing along to the entirety of Alanis Morissette's *Jagged Little Pill*. Make sure you really focus on screaming the entire album, with "You Oughta Know" repeated at least five times. (For lesbians, Melissa Etheridge's *Skin* should also be added to the rotation.)

- Have a good cry, followed by a good scream into a pillow. Repeat as needed.

- Wipe your social media of any proof that your ex ever existed. You will thank Today You when Future You doesn't have to see their obnoxious mug pop up in your Facebook memories every damn day for the rest of your life.

- Have your way with some really ill-advised online shopping. Delight in joy when purchasing and also when the presents appear on your doorstep as if delivered by the Dopamine Fairy. Repeat as financially feasible.

- You know that thing you never did or ate or watched because your ex didn't like that thing? Do that thing. Do all those things. Perhaps have Alanis playing while doing the things. Multitask.

- Purge. This can look different for everyone. Purge anything your ex ever gave you (unless that thing is valuable, then maybe go with Pawn instead of Purge), anything in your house that has a bad memory associated with it, any photos that make your skin crawl. Anything that will feel out of place in your future Zen life—purge that shit.

   (Note: Sometimes this purging can mean actually getting rid of items, sometimes it can mean lighting them on fire à la *Waiting to Exhale*'s Angela Bassett. But sometimes it can simply mean gathering up all the stuff, putting it in a few boxes, and storing it out of sight, or even off-site. Not because you aren't ready to move on, but because sometimes we can regret the fires we light when in a heightened emotional state. At the very least purge the items from your line of sight for the time being, giving yourself enough emotional space to decide if you really want to resort to destruction in the future.)

DIVORCE SQUAD

When I Knew It Was Over

"We'd been married about eight years, about the time the luster starts to come off the marriage. You still love her, but you are starting to know a little too much about each other. In an effort to reignite that spark she and I took a romantic vacation to Mexico. It was beautiful and luxurious, for all intents and purposes it should have been a really nice vacation.

"I was out on the beach one day, in the private cabana I had arranged, and I noticed my wife approaching me. She had a scowl on her face as she approached. She said, 'Is this what you do all day?'

"I asked her where she had been, it was almost noon. She said, 'Where have I been? The same place I've been every morning, taking a shit. Because since the day I got here, I've done nothing but piss out of my ass.' She grunted and sat down and began to complain about the heat.

"We had no children, we had everything going well in our lives, we had money to burn, great friends, amazing family, good health. But it was in that instant, that one brief, three-minute encounter, that something changed inside me. Within two years I packed one single small suitcase with a couple work shirts and a couple pants. About a thousand dollars in cash we had stashed at home. And I walked out the front door. And I never walked back."

....

"He was an electrician. When we were first married, I was so worried every day when he left for work. I just wanted him to come home safe. Toward the end . . . I thought things would be so much easier if he had an accident and didn't make it home."

....

"We were at Disneyland and had a huge fight because I wanted to buy an $8 bottle of water. He asked for a divorce when we got home from the vacation."

....

"I wanted out of my marriage so I met with a therapist and asked her if I was maybe having a mental break-down or a midlife crisis."

....

"I'm twenty-three and lying in bed with my thirty-one-year-old husband watching Rick Steves's *Europe* before we fall asleep. I turn to my husband and say with all sincerity, 'I can't wait to travel around Europe with you.' He replies without looking at me, almost spitting: 'We're not going to Europe . . . There's enough to see here in our own country.'

That was the moment.

I don't know if it was how quickly he responded, or how matter-of-factly he said it, or the small-mindedness it represented, but it was a singular moment that changed something for me. I slowly turned my gaze back toward Rick, removed my hand from his arm, and thought 'Fuuuuuuuuuuuuuuuuck. I married the wrong guy.'"

2

Divorce Announcements Should Be a Thing

(the most efficient ways to let everyone know that your life has been blown up)

The people in your life have received the wedding announcement, the baby announcements, and they are now getting the divorce announcement. It's the circle of life, really.

But how exactly do you announce this less than celebratory milestone? On the one hand, it's really nobody's business what is going on in your life or in your marriage. So maybe you don't need to announce it at all. But on the other hand, situations like chatting with another parent at your kid's baseball practice or catching up with your uncle at Thanksgiving dinner can get real awkward real fast if no one has been made aware that your marriage has imploded.

So. It's probably best to get the word out somehow, because Lord knows that Thanksgiving is already awkward enough without news of your marital upheaval being passed around with the cranberry sauce.

When it came time to let people know about my divorce, I realized I had previous experience with this kind of information spreading. I didn't come out of the closet until I was thirty years old, so I had quite a long contact list to get through on my "Hey! I'm Gay!" announcement tour. I started small, a lunch with a couple friends, dinner with a couple more. I was nervous and self-conscious about what my friends would think or say. I called people up for heart-to-heart discussions about my sexuality. I sent awkward emails to the family members I was scared to tell in person. This went on and on and on, until I eventually lost interest in this tedious project. One time I took Elizabeth to a party with me, where I knew a large group of friends would be in attendance. I walked up to one of my friends and said, "This is Elizabeth, we are dating. As in gay. As in I'm gay. Spread the word to the rest of the party please." Then I headed to the appetizer table, because by that point I was much more interested in spinach dip than having any more heart-to-heart coming-out discussions.

When announcing my divorce, I skipped all the one-on-one chats and went straight to covering as much ground as possible. My close friends and family knew what was going on, but who has time to individually alert everyone on the contact list? I had done a fall photoshoot with the kids, where I made a point to get plenty of photos with just the three of us. The photos came out great, so I posted them to my social media. Then I sent a Christmas card to my friends and family that only included the kids and me. And then I answered a lot of concerned, questioning texts, "So, um, is Elizabeth just camera shy or . . ."

I gotta say, I highly recommend going the divorce announcement route if you can manage to plan your split around the holidays. (Although "Happy Spring! I'm Divorced!" works too.) I was able to cover a lot of ground with one simple card, and anyone who wasn't on my Christmas card list found out from the grapevine, saving me a whole lot of effort. Done and done. On to the spinach dip.

Now that I think about it, being gay and being divorced are similar in that you end up having to repeatedly come out as both. "What does your husband do for a living?" "Uh, well, I'm divorced. And he's a woman. I'll add you to the Christmas card list so you can stay updated."

Divorce Announcement Options

People send baby announcements to let everyone know about their adorable new addition, so why not normalize sending divorce announcements to alert the masses to our delightful subtraction? Let us count the ways this can be done.

Social Media Post

You really can't beat the reach of a social media post when it comes to spreading information quickly (see also: conspiracy theories). Facebook seems to be the social media outlet that includes the most friends and family members (see also: your crazy uncle who only posts conspiracy theories), so it's a great place to get the word out efficiently.

If you go the Facebook route you have a few options for how exactly you can execute the reveal. You can go with the fan favorite **Scorched Earth**, wherein you burn your ex to the ground with a searingly honest account of what the fuck is going on in your disaster of a marriage. I highly recommend not doing this, although I absolutely delight in reading these types of posts when they pop up. You can also go with the always interesting **Breadcrumbs** posts that gradually reveal more and more clues for your social media followers to piece together. Maybe photos of your new place, or several photos that pointedly do not include your ex, or hashtags having to do with self-discovery and new beginnings. Let the internet sleuths put in some work to figure out your news. You'll probably even end up the topic of a group text where friends work together to decipher what is going on in your life. Another popular Facebook option is the **Inspirational Quotes** route. Simply scour the interwebs for memes of quotes that speak to your current state of mind. Post any and all of them. Your contacts will figure out the rest.

You can also use Instagram for both the **Breadcrumbs** and **Inspirational Quotes** route. Lean heavily into outing yourself through overtly single-looking images and ridiculously artistic interpretations of introspective quotes.

If you are feeling modern, there's always the possibility of putting together a solid TikTok to make your announcement. Maybe a quick dance routine and lip-sync to "I Will Survive"? Or "Since You've Been Gone"? Or "We Are Never Getting Back Together"? Perhaps a medley?

Group Text

Maybe throw all your important folks on a group text and let everyone know at the same time, "Hello! I'm getting divorced! Wanted you to know. I'm fine. Kids are fine. I don't need anything, thanks for asking."

Holiday Card

Obviously this is my personal favorite. Set up a photoshoot with a good photographer. Get your hair done and find yourself a cute outfit. Make sure the kids are adorable too. Then let good lighting and Photoshop editing tools produce some excellent "I'm divorced and doing great!" photos for your holiday Splitsville card.

Friend Who Can't Keep a Secret

We all know exactly which of our friends and family can't keep a secret for shit. Call them up, tell them all about your divorce. Then let them do the heavy lifting of alerting everyone else. (Maybe ask them to keep it quiet, so you know for sure that the message will spread the second you hang up the phone.)

Don't Bother

Another option is to just let it all ride. Tell a few close friends and family members what is going on, and then let everyone else figure it out during awkward conversations at baseball practice or Thanksgiving dinner. Have fun with it by making up new, increasingly outlandish divorce stories to tell each new person you have to inform, "We thought we were each boring suburban parents, but it turns out we were both undercover secret agents. It was too much to overcome, as you can imagine."

DIVORCE SQUAD

Divorce Announcements

"I burst into tears at one point while at work, so I had to start telling people why I was a basket case. For the rest of the world, I posted a picture on Facebook of the new house and mentioned that daddy was down the street. Then I got A LOT of Facebook messages. I had an old roommate get offended that I didn't personally text her."

....

"I told my family and close friends and let it go from there. Word spread pretty quickly."

....

"I was a media personality and stopped mentioning my wife on air or in print. With months of getting questions, my boss finally allowed me thirty seconds on air to clarify my marital situation. That message included that while my marriage was dissolving, both my ex-wife and I were more firmly committed to our children than ever."

3

Blowing Things Up

(and putting them back together)

Elizabeth and I spent years navigating to the end of our marriage; we circled and circled around our divorce, getting close, pulling back, approaching again, moving forward, backward, sideways.

In an effort to keep our split moving smoothly, I went along with pretty much anything my ex suggested. I was the one who wanted the divorce, so I felt like I owed it to her to keep the details as simple as possible. She refused to move out of the house, so I agreed to be the one who left. Elizabeth wasn't very attached to the family home, so it was understood that she would eventually find a place she liked, and I would be allowed to move back in at that time. (Why on earth we thought this was a good plan, I still do not know.)

We also owned several rental properties together and agreed to keep joint ownership of the properties post-split. We were even going to maintain our joint bank account for any property or kid expenses. (Another plan that was lacking in logic.)

I moved out and got settled into my new place, and we slowly started figuring out our life post-split. Because of COVID, even after I moved out, I was still at our family home doing virtual home school with the kids every day. Our money was still intertwined, because we had so many moving parts in our financial life. My ex would regularly let herself into my new house unannounced; she had a garage door opener and a key. I was still cooking and cleaning at our family home every day when I was there doing school with the kids. And I was still the person Elizabeth texted when she was stressed out or upset.

So, as you can see, we were not doing a super-great job *actually separating* during the first couple of months of our separation. But I was still just trying to keep everything copacetic and not make any sudden movements that might hurt Elizabeth or the kids. I didn't want an explosion.

But as it turns out, divorce, no matter why or how it happens, is a life explosion. You are taking a family unit and shaking it up like a snow globe. There's no way to really know how and when all the flying pieces will settle back down to earth. And in the meantime, you are going to be a bit discombobulated by the wreckage.

In many cases, divorce can feel like an actual explosion, because a huge cataclysmic event is what triggered the beginning of the end. A few of my Divorce Squad felt like their ex essentially walked in one day and announced that their marriage was over. No prior head's up, just—boom—everything exploded into bits. That kind of destruction can be especially difficult, because you are left to contend with a mess someone else created, one you may have even tried really hard to avoid.

Even in the best-case scenario, where two people simply decide to consciously uncouple, there is still a significant change in the family equation to contend with. You've gone from a couple living together to two people doing life solo. Or a couple living with kids, to two people in two different homes, navigating co-parenting together . . . while apart. The change in the equation, even in the best-case situation, is rattling. And let's be honest, most divorces don't fall into anything resembling the best-case category.

As I mentioned, I'd gone pretty much numb by the end of my relationship. But even before that I'd always been a pretty chill person. I don't waver too much from the middle of the road when it comes to emotions. Never too happy, never too sad, never too angry. I'm basically like a stoned person most of the time (munchies and all). Even after I moved out and our split was official . . . still not much going on in the feelings category.

Overall, we had pretty much avoided anything resembling an explosion during our separation. Look at us go.

But then.

A few months after I moved out of the house, Elizabeth told me that she had met someone and was in love.

Cue the explosion.

I went a little nuts. And everyone in my life went a little concerned. I've never been big on emotions, and for some reason Elizabeth's announcement brought out *all* my emotions. It was confusing, to say the least, especially to me.

After years and years of moving forward, backward, and sideways, Elizabeth's new relationship meant we were done. Finally done. But in all the time we'd spent slowly getting to the end, I had never considered how I would feel when we finally got there. I think I always assumed, since I was the one who initiated the split, that the end would be nothing more than a relief. But, in reality, the end became the beginning of something much more complicated. It was the beginning of really processing our years together and also being forced to really contend with what it was going to mean to lose half my time with the kids.

After pushing everything down for so long, there was something about the end that caused everything to come all the way back up. I could feel my numb state thawing at a rate that felt unmanageable, and I knew in my gut I couldn't remain as entwined with my ex as we'd planned while constructing our split.

Another person might have just calmly articulated this change in comfort level. But going from numb to flurrying emotions left me feeling crazy, and apparently, I thought leaning into that feeling was the way to go. So, I took all the things we had so carefully constructed for so many years.

And I blew them the f up.

I filed for divorce and pushed for mediation to split up all of our assets. I told Elizabeth I was no longer willing to wait around until she was ready to move out of the family home, I was done waiting for her to be ready, I needed to start my new life. I had already waited years and years.

All this absolutely shocked Elizabeth. Why couldn't we keep things the way they were? Why on earth had I agreed to everything we put together if I was just going to blow it all up? Why did I think it was okay to break all the promises we had made simply because she was dating someone new? Why was I being so crazy?

At the time, I didn't have much of an explanation for what I was doing; I just knew it all had to be done. I knew that I couldn't keep up with the arrangement we had. I didn't want to be entangled anymore. I wanted to be free. And I wanted it now. No more waiting, no more pushing things back, no more. It needed to happen. Now. After years of dragging our feet, we managed to wrap up our divorce agreement in about a month. We were done and I needed our union to be done as well.

Elizabeth did not take my sudden change of heart well. And so began the phase of our split when everything in the snow globe was officially shaken to shit. Screaming matches became our primary form of communication. We nearly broke the mediator during our first meeting. She introduced her new girlfriend to our kids eleven days after telling me about the relationship. I threatened to evict her cousin who had moved into our family home after I left. She left the house needing thousands of dollars in repairs when she moved out. I pushed, she pulled, we both raged and raged.

It took us almost a year to get to the other side of this explosion that I caused. I'd broken Elizabeth's trust and I'd broken everything else too. We'd spent years trying to avoid the ugliness I brought into the mix. Despite everything that led to our divorce, Elizabeth didn't deserve the way I acted at the end, and frankly I didn't deserve it either. I should have been better for both of us. It all could have been avoided if I had just said, "Oh, you met someone? Cool, I'm super happy for you." Things could have continued on as they were, and nothing would have had to change.

But then I remember, things really, really needed to change. We really, really needed a legitimate separation, not the dance we were doing after I moved out. We needed the space and freedom to start new versions of our lives, and that was never going to happen with the two of us in the same house every day, intertwined in each other's lives as much as we were.

At the time, blowing everything up felt like the only way to get where we needed to go. Being slow and deliberate had not served us well at all.

Building new things means getting rid of all the remnants of old things. It has to be done. Blowing up a life is an extraordinary opportunity to put things back together in better ways, even if it can feel scary as shit when it is happening. Even if you never wanted the explosion in the first place.

My biggest regret when it comes to my own explosion is that I wasn't mature enough to handle my swirling emotions in a less hurtful way, that I didn't work harder to get where we needed to go and still protect those around me from my internal chaos. But that is my rational brain judging a very irrational time in my life. My rational brain hasn't quite forgiven my irrational behavior.

That irrational time had severe long-term consequences in our divorce. My behavior those few months after our split became our one and only story post-divorce. The previous twelve years of relationship nuance were replaced with the singular narrative: "Dawn is crazy." There was no grace, there was no forgiveness, and that's probably exactly what I deserved. That new narrative has permeated our co-parenting relationship in a way that completely altered what we are or can be. I still haven't decided whether that is a good or bad thing.

Changing the shape of things can get messy. No matter who wanted or caused the explosion, everyone is hit with debris. No one gets out of this unscathed. And no one is delighting to be left with nothing but charred remains of an entire life.

Maybe this isn't where you thought you would be, maybe it's not where you think you want to be. But the good news is, this is a temporary state.

Try to remember that fact as you navigate your explosion. How you feel in the middle of the chaos is not your new normal; it's just the armor you've put on to survive the blast. Emotions will be high (and they should be!), decisions will be rash, but consequences will be long term. Do an occasional gut check before making any hasty choices. Ask yourself, "Is this the story I want to be told about me? Is this the story I want to tell about myself?"

No matter where you are on your particular journey, I hope you can see, or maybe just imagine, a place not far down the road where things are better. I know that might sound completely out of the realm of possibility right now, but I promise, it's waiting for you. A time when all the scattered pieces have found their place to rest, in their new shape. When you realize that all the mess was necessary to build you back stronger and better than you ever thought possible. It's all waiting for you just up the (possibly very, very bumpy) road. I promise.

Post-Explosion Dos and Don'ts

A life explosion can be very confounding. Things have gone ass over teakettle, and you aren't sure which way is up. You aren't sure of anything at all. And that's okay. You don't need all the answers today, or even tomorrow. (Next week isn't looking super promising either.) What you need is to plant your feet and hold on as your new normal starts to settle into place. Don't make any sudden movements, don't make any ill-advised purchases, *don't call your hairdresser*. Take a deep breath and trust that it's going to be okay eventually.

Don't

Buy/sell something big (*let's try to keep the credit rating from being exploded as well*)

Text/call the ex and share your emotional turmoil (*just don't*)

Lose your temper (*with your ex, your kids, or the asshole driving fifty miles an hour in the fast lane on the freeway*)

Get into a serious relationship (*don't bring another poor soul into this shit show*)

Get bangs (*you'll scare the children*)

Do

Get some therapy (*probably lots of therapy*)

Call/get together with your friends (*this counts as therapy too*)

Rage journal (*the page will gather up all your anger and keep it safe for you*)

Make out with a stranger (*live a little*)

Start going on walks or runs, followed by ordering takeout (*balance*)

DIVORCE SQUAD

Boom

"I spent months planning. I rented an apartment without him knowing. I set it up with furniture that looked like our house, so the kids would be comfortable. I started buying double of everything at the grocery store, and kept items under my desk at work. I was getting ready. Then I went home one day and told him I was leaving. He freaked out and told me I couldn't, he wouldn't let me. I took the kids and left. I didn't hear from him for weeks."

....

"She'd been cheating on me for six months and I knew about it. I was still willing to stay and make it work because we had kids. I was raised to believe divorce was just not something people did. She said she was leaving and I told her if she walked out of our house, she was never allowed back in. It was her choice and she left. I think at that moment she was dead to me, there was no going back."

....

"My wife had been struggling mentally for a long time. One day, after all this time, she said she wanted to split up. A few months later she had moved in with a guy who she had always told me was just a friend."

....

"I found out my husband had been sleeping with my best friend. Our kids were three and five years old. He blew up everything."

FUCK YOU, YOU FUCKING FUCK
(A TIME FOR JOURNALING)

We've now reached the interactive portion of our program.

As I mentioned in the previous chapter, sometimes the heightened emotions of divorce can lead us to actions or decisions that turn out to have less than awesome long-term consequences. Our emotions can explode in ways that leave us feeling a little like we've gone on a bender and are now left to contend with the mess we made when we were not in our right state of mind.

There's a reason why every one of my Divorce Squad laughed when I mentioned writing a book about divorce with every chapter titled "Fuck You, You Fucking Fuck." And that reason is because, for all of our efforts to be civil, mature, well-adjusted adults, at our core "Fuck You, You Fucking Fuck" speaks very clearly to our overall feelings about divorce. Our apologies to Zen.

Most likely, "Fuck You, You Fucking Fuck" speaks to you as well. And instead of pushing that feeling down, I think we need to bring it right up to the surface. Trust me when I tell you it is going to make its way to the surface in some way or another eventually, so I recommend getting out in front of the excavation.

Instead of exploding your "Fuck You" all over your ex or other people in your life, let's start with exploding all over a journal. It may sound silly, but emotions need an outlet, and rage journaling is actually a really great way to emote safely. So grab some paper and a pen, and let's start digging.

There are no rules for this journaling, other than you should write down exactly what you are feeling: the good, the bad, and especially the ugly. Keep writing as you run into these prompts throughout the book, and continue writing every time you feel yourself about to go on an emotional bender. You'll find the release cathartic and sometimes simply getting the rage out of your head can free up space for other, less irritable thoughts. At the very least, it is probably better to release onto these pages instead of innocent bystanders who happen across your path on an off day.

So, off we go!

For this first entry, let's keep it simple. Finish this sentence. (Feel free to take up as many journals as you need to finish this sentence.)

FUCK YOU, YOU FUCKING FUCK . . . _____

_____

_____

_____

_____

_____

_____

4

Moving On and Moving Out

(what happens when one home becomes two)

While you are married, your house can come to represent a lot of different things. It could be the place you designed from the ground up or maybe remodeled together. It could be the place the two of you brought your babies home, where you built your family from scratch. Its walls may hold all your memories, from the framed pictures to the truths they've absorbed over the years. But in the end, your house might just feel like little more than the place where you failed to pull off your plans of forever.

When you separated from your spouse your housing situation most likely went one of three ways: (1) Both partners moved out of the house into new places. (2) You moved out and your spouse stayed. (3) Your ex moved out and you stayed.

However the housing situation unfolds, it can inevitably become a very literal representation of your marriage being dismantled. For instance, one of my Divorce Squad was cheated on and then left in an almost empty house after the split: "She took damn near all the furniture when she left, including my bed. I went into the garage and found this old folding table and used it as my dining table. She literally and figuratively emptied me out."

I'm not sure I can think of a more fitting image than that of a newly divorced person sitting at a folding table, in the middle of their emptied-out living room, surveying what is left of the life that used to exist within those walls. That's some high art right there.

Ever the innovators, Elizabeth and I skipped all of the above and went with Option 4, in which we "broke up" but both stayed in the home, living in different rooms, so that we didn't have to be away from our kids. This is by far the worst of all the options. What can I say, I'm an overachiever in all things, including self-destruction.

I firmly believe Option 4 should be recognized as an official ring of hell. Do I send my petition directly to the Vatican? Option 4 is when you know that your marriage is toast, but for various reasons you decide to continue to cohabitate. You move into different rooms of the house and pretend that everything is fine. TOTALLY FINE. I'm pretty sure this setup has been the basis for a sitcom. Although I'm also pretty sure nothing about this setup is remotely funny.

I remember trying to justify the situation to friends, "Look, my kids are the loves of my life, and I want to be with them every day. If that means also living with a person I can't stand, then that's a small price to pay."

The looks on my friends' faces should have shaken me back to reality. Confused expressions, raised eyebrows, reluctant head nodding, "Uh . . . okay. But, are you *sure* that's the best idea?"

It was not the best idea. It put us in a weird holding pattern between marriage and divorce, a purgatory where I convinced myself that I was treading water, when really my ass was drowning more and more every day.

It was, indeed, the worst of ideas.

When we finally split up, I had the unique opportunity to experience what it feels like to leave the family home and also what it feels like to be the one who stays. Both situations were aggressively odd.

We purchased our home as a new build, watched it being constructed, and picked out every detail of its design. I loved our house. But more importantly, it just felt like our kids' home. I was breaking up their family; I really, really didn't want them to lose their home too. So I was adamant that we keep the house post-split.

When we split up, I moved into a place that was literally forty-five seconds away from our family home, with the agreement that I would move back once Elizabeth found a new place that she liked. But I still had to be over at the main house pretty much every day doing COVID home school with the kids.

Being in the house when I didn't live there anymore was very, very odd.

The house had been my home for six years—I'd built the damn thing. And now I was standing in the kitchen, but it was no longer my kitchen, but I was still there taking care of the kids, but I would be leaving later in the day, because I didn't live there anymore. I belonged there because my kids were there, but I didn't belong there because I had broken up their family. It was a continuous hokey pokey dance of emotions any time I was in the house.

I still loved that house. I still loved being with my kids in the house. I loved the animals that were in the house. I loved just about everything about the place, except the fact that my ex lived there. So, I simply had to put my head down and wait until she was ready to move out, so that I could move back in. Hokey pokey.

When Elizabeth told me she had met someone and was in love a few months after I moved out, one of my first reactions was, "Great, get out of my house."

That seems a little cold, I know, and Elizabeth thought so too. But I had been the one to leave the house in order to keep the peace and give her time to figure out her next move. She was in love—next move figured out. Now, let's get this party started.

We headed to mediation and I got the house in an asset split. I gave her six months to get out but pushed her to vacate sooner. For some reason that house represented something very big to me and not being in my home left me feeling completely untethered.

The many moving parts of getting me back into my house involved me selling my new place and becoming a teensy bit homeless while I waited for Elizabeth to vacate our family home.

So, because this was a particularly sane period of my life, I put all my stuff in storage and moved into a hotel for two months. Kinda like a rock star, or Lindsay Lohan. Except a lot less drugs and a lot more kids doing virtual school on the sofa bed.

The hotel was an extended stay place that was essentially an apartment, with a bedroom, living room, and a little kitchen. I could wrap up my workday at the desk and then roll two feet over to the table for dinner. The convenience!

The other hotel guests included traveling families, actual homeless people who were looking for a place to rest for a while, and entire youth sports teams who were visiting for various tournaments. There was one woman who appeared to be training for some sort of athletic event with her coach. She could be found sprinting through the parking lot every morning. And every morning two men who did not know this woman would lean against the bumper of their car, smoking cigarettes, watching her run.

The hotel allowed pets, so there were dogs, cats, lizards, and turtles roaming the halls. One lady walked around all day with a parakeet on her shoulder. Many of the guests decided that a room with a kitchen the size of an airplane bathroom was just the place for them to experiment with cooking exotic foods. Which left the hallways thick with a not so appetizing assortment of smells. It was an eclectic place, to say the least.

The kids were good sports and didn't complain about being cooped up in the small space. My son would excitedly tell everyone, "We have a couch . . . that turns into a BED!" We were right next to a mall, so we'd ride our scooters over there and get ice cream and smoothies often. It was like the world's longest vacation, in the world's least exciting destination. And there I sat, once again waiting, on the last leg of my years-long journey to being divorced.

Finally, Elizabeth moved out of the house, and I was able to get back in. I had been gone for less than a year, but the space felt almost foreign when I came back. A different version of me had lived there previously, and I wasn't quite sure how this new me would fit in the home. I moved all my stuff back in, put new paint on the walls, and lightened up the kitchen with a new backsplash and bright cabinets.

It is a very big house. And it felt very, very empty when the kids weren't home. I'd never been in the home without them, which made their absence even heavier. Every corner held a memory of a different life. Bringing dates over felt like cheating. I wondered if it was really possible to build something new on top of the rubble of something that had been so broken.

I made an effort to spend as much time as possible in the house with the kids. We played and crafted and swam and watched movies and snuggled with abandon. I wanted this home to start representing good times, instead of just being the place where their family had fallen apart.

For months after I moved back in, I found myself waiting for the garage door to slam, waiting for Elizabeth to come spinning into my peaceful space. Before our split, I would make dinner every night, and as I was cooking, I would brace myself for Elizabeth coming home. The garage door would slam as she came in the house, and my body would instantly tense up. I would take a deep breath and mentally prepare for having to do the next few hours with her.

After I moved back in, I was still tense because that was how I had always been in that home. My body didn't quite know how to be anything else just yet.

And then a few months after I moved back the garage door slammed one night while I was making dinner. It was the kids running into the house. As they came bounding into the kitchen, I realized the slamming hadn't sent an instant dread to my gut; I was no longer tense. My body had finally relaxed, and the house had slowly started feeling like a home again. I had put down my roots, set up the space like I wanted, and finally created what I'd always longed for—peace. Uninterrupted, unfiltered, unedited . . . peace.

••••

Whether you leave or stay in your family home, you are going to go through a period of figuring out exactly how your post-divorce life looks in your place of residence. I highly recommend really taking the time to settle into your new place, or resettle into your family home if you are the one who stays. Be deliberate about making your space feel comfortable and bright and explicitly YOU. It can actually be unexpectedly difficult to figure out what is unequivocally YOU after years spent being part of a WE.

Rediscover who you are and what you like. Go to a home goods store and roam the aisles, look online at different decoration ideas, keep a photo album on your phone titled "My Style." Put images in that album that feel good. And then fill your home with those things. You don't have to spend a fortune, and some of the work can be done by simply getting rid of old shit you know you *don't* like. I'm here to tell you that a solid purge never hurt a living space.

Finding peace in your home is one of the most important steps to finding it in the rest of your life post-divorce. But, like everything else, it's going to take time. Be patient with yourself as you acclimate to your new living situation, wherever it happens to be. Give yourself time to recover from the wreckage before expecting tranquility to come bounding in the door.

At the beginning you will feel like that divorced person sitting at a folding table in the middle of their emptied-out living room, in the middle of their emptied-out life. That space isn't going to be Pinterest-ready for a really long time. And that's okay. First, you sit at the folding table and cry. Then you get up and figure out how you want to fill the space: what colors, what furniture, what art. Then as you are placing these new things, you will be putting down seeds. Slowly, sometimes infuriatingly slowly, a new life will start to grow. And then eventually that space, and who you are in that space, will become something completely different. Something you never could have imagined while sitting at that folding table.

It's okay if you are still at the folding table right now and haven't quite gotten past the crying phase. You'll get up soon, and the seeds are ready when you are.

As you settle into your new home, and your new life, always remember that a home is never just a collection of walls. It sounds cheesy as shit, but home exists wherever your people are, and wherever those people are safe and happy. I learned this when I watched my kids delight at being able to set up a *Floor Is Lava* game that covered every square inch of our tiny hotel room. They were unphased that we were living in a shoebox. They were happy, I was happy, and all was well. Because peace doesn't need much square footage to grow.

DIVORCE SQUAD
Change of Address

"We sold the house. I really wrestled with that decision. But this was our family house, we built a life there, we lived there for four years, we brought the baby home there, all that stuff. That is really what I needed to leave behind."

....

"My ex still lives in the house we shared. I think about one of two things when I'm over there. One, I miss that fucking pool, it's fucking fantastic. And two, she has no pictures of me up in the house. So, when I'm over there I'll excuse myself and go into one of my kids' rooms, I'll grab a picture that they have of me in their room, I'll put it under my arm, and before I leave, I'll place it where I know she's not going to see it for a day or so. She's never said anything, but the kids have mentioned it. I do it all the time. A little representation would be nice!"

....

"I'm the one that stayed in our house. I think I would have had a really hard time if my ex-wife stayed and her new boyfriend moved in. I know it was not easy for her when my fiancé moved in."

....

"It was weird, I was just so happy to be away from the emotional abuse et cetera that I didn't miss my huge house at all. My daughter loved her room at my apartment and she felt similar to me—it was just so peaceful!! Neither of us looked back and have not been back for almost two years."

5

The Seven Stages of Divorce

*(kind of like the five stages of grief but
with a lot more alcohol and takeout)*

One of the first therapists I spoke to post-divorce was all about equating my journey to that of someone who had experienced a death. She said that the end of a marriage was a death of sorts and I was going to go through the five stages of grief as a result: denial, anger, bargaining, depression, and acceptance. The grief diagnosis was a bit off the mark for me at that time because I felt like I had already done an awful lot of grieving for our marriage when it started dying years prior to our split. But, that being said, she did get me thinking about the actual stages of divorce and what they look like for different people.

Now that I have made my way through my divorce, it seems to me that grief might be too classy of a metaphor for the process. Perhaps something involving chaos, injuries, and general confusion may have more in common with divorce than grief. And where better to find that combo platter than reality TV?

On the game show *Wipeout* contestants run around an obstacle course doing increasingly ridiculous physical challenges that almost always result in said contestant face-planting into a pool of mud. They start out on the obstacle course with people throwing big balls at them, trying to knock them off already shaky ground, then they cross a tiny ledge in front of a wall that has a hundred mechanical fists randomly punching out. Inevitably one of the fists catches the poor contestant in the gut and they are punched into a pit filled with mud. The next challenge is to cross over a pool of water by bouncing on the top of four huge red balls. No one ever makes it past the first ball. Instead, they bounce on it, lose their footing, violently face-plant into the second ball, and belly flop into the water. Then they have to swim to a ladder, climb out, and throw themselves at another big ball, resulting in more face-plants / flops / future physical therapy. Then they drag themselves out of the water one last time and pump their arms in the air at the finish line. They have survived. They have a concussion and mud in all sorts of unfortunate places . . . but they have survived.

As you make your way through your stages of divorce, you are going to feel a lot like a contestant on *Wipeout*, completely battered and generally off balance.

Unlike a *Wipeout* obstacle course, there are no rules as to when you will hit the various stages of divorce or in what order you will hit them. For added fun, there is a good chance you'll visit each stage more than once; sometimes you may even be lucky enough to visit more than one in a single day. The good news is, you'll make it to the end, you will. But you are going to have to dodge a lot of hits and will probably get some mud in unfortunate places along the way. What an exciting time this is!

As you travel through your post-divorce obstacle course, it's important to keep the attitude of a *Wipeout* contestant. Those fools just never stay down. Ball to the gut, they keep going; fist to the eye socket, there's no stopping; debilitating concussion, just shake it off.

Like those contestants, you are going to incur some injuries and setbacks throughout your stages of divorce, and you are going to need to brush everything off and keep going, because there's more mud to conquer and sweet relief waiting for you at the finish line.

Ready, Set, Go!

Your Post-Divorce Obstacle Course
Denial

Yes, I stole the denial stage from grief, because any decent life journey usually starts with a healthy amount of denial that the journey is necessary at all. In the case of divorce, the denial stage can start years before the breakup even takes place, with you repeatedly dodging the reality that your marriage is toast.

Even once you move past the initial denial that divorce is imminent, there is still room for this stage to linger. Maybe you are dodging the reality that your "trial" separation is actually a "forever and ever, this shit is all the way over" separation. Maybe you are in denial about your role in the way everything went down. Maybe you are excited to finally be done and are in complete denial about the many obstacles you still have left to navigate.

Which leads us to . . .

Glee/Booze

Your disaster of a union is over! Finally! You are free! Someone cue Helen Reddy and gather up the champagne glasses! We are in the fun stage!

Now, I realize not everyone lands on this stage, and some people may be the opposite of elated at the ending of their marriage. If that is the case, you might still be forced into this stage by friends who show up at your door with booze and/or ice cream, insisting that you are better off without your cheating, lying, no good, very bad ex. They will be asking you to deny your heartbreak and lean into celebrating your freedom from someone who clearly didn't deserve you.

I recommend enjoying this stage, even if you have to fake the fun; go out to drinks, high-five with abandon, buy a couple of new outfits. It's an entertaining phase. Unfortunately, it's also usually a relatively short phase, with many a face-plant on the horizon.

Blame Game

Ah, the reality of our divorce obstacle course. This is when we reach the wall of repeated punches to the gut. Things can start to feel heavy when the day-to-day motions of this new life expose what reality is going to look like going forward.

We miss our kids. We miss half of our bank account. We miss having someone to talk to. We miss all the things our partner did around the house, even if we don't necessarily miss our partner being around the house.

And, because we are still pretty early in our journey, we aren't quite ready to get into the depths of what this hurt is all about. Instead, we get defensive, we deflect, we blame.

All this is our ex's fault. All of it. If they hadn't been all the horrible things that they were, if they hadn't done all the horrible things that they did, none of this would be happening, and none of these things would hurt. It is ALL THEIR FAULT and they are ASSHOLES.

The anger of the blame game stage shares some origins with the denial stage, because we are still generally opposed to owning our part in our divorce and getting to the root of emotions is not on the docket just yet. We are hurt and irritated and pointing fingers with vigor.

We look a bit like a *Wipeout* contestant right before they jump toward their first big red ball; when they really, really believe there is a chance they are going to bounce on top of all four of the balls and safely land on the other side of the pool completely dry.

We are not in a super-realistic frame of mind.

Netflix and Cry

The Netflix and Cry portion of the program is when we hit the first red ball. Our legs buckle, we smash off the second ball, and we go splat into the pool below. We get drenched in what is really going on in our lives, and we are no longer able to ignore it.

We curl up on the couch, binge-watch forty-six hours of questionable programming, and cry into our Chinese takeout containers. It might be the first time we've really cried. It might be scarier than we thought it would be. It's definitely the beginning of being honest about what has really taken place.

All the Therapy

Once you've had your way with Netflix and you've recovered from your crying-induced migraine, it might be time to start googling some therapists. You've finally hit your breaking point, so now it's time to get to work putting things back together. (Please see also Chapter 6, "All the Therapy.")

For the record, I think the therapy stage is a welcome addition to any of the stages listed here, but I tend to believe you might not quite be ready to do the real work until you've embraced the sadness of your new reality.

Ho Phase

Sure, therapy is great, and leaning into the healing is going to serve us very well in the future. But all that is long-term shit. In the meantime, let's have a little fun.

And so, we now enter our Ho Phase. In this phase we are like a *Wipeout* contestant who has a wardrobe malfunction post-bounce and goes flying through the air with a boob hanging out. What fun!

I firmly believe the Ho Phase is an important stage of your divorce journey. Sure, it's superficial and maybe a little immature, but it's also FUN. It's fun to go out and do simple things. To have one thing in your life that doesn't feel heavy and sad and overwhelmingly BIG. There's nothing big about meeting up with an attractive person, agreeing that you are both looking for something casual, and then tearing each other's clothes off.

There's no commitment or deep feelings or anything that has decades of past or future associated with it. It's just two bodies exploring. You've probably been with only your ex for a really long time. You got into your routines, you knew what buttons to push, you went through the motions. With new people you can try new tricks and learn new moves. If you're lucky these new people might even teach you a few new things about your own body. All with absolutely no strings attached. (Unless you want to experiment with attaching strings? Go for it!)

The Shrug

The final stage of divorce is not as deep as acceptance, which is the final stage of grief. Acceptance feels big and final and evolved. I'm not sure we need to get that far to really make our way through our stages of divorce.

One of my favorite quotes that I revisited often during my divorce is this: "The opposite of love isn't hate; the opposite of love is indifference." The hate you carry around at the beginning of your divorce is rooted in the love that used to exist between the two of you. As long as you hate your ex, you are still admitting that you care an awful lot. Caring is not something that is easy to navigate around and through, but once you do, you'll find that indifference is such an easier place to reside.

And to me nothing signifies indifference quite like a solid shoulder shrug.

You'll know you've made your way to the other side of your divorce drama when you ex's bullshittery no longer sends you into a tailspin. You hear it, you absorb it, and you shrug. Because you're done with the blaming and the anger and the tears. You've realized your ex is no longer worth the energy any of those things require.

So, you shrug.

And you hold your arms up in victory at the finish line (after you tuck your boob back into your shirt).

6

All the Therapy

*(when your friends are officially tired
of listening to your bullshit)*

I tried a lot of different therapy at a lot of different times throughout my divorce. We tried couple's therapy before we split, we
tried co-parenting therapy after we split, and I did individual
therapy with a few therapists along the way. I had mixed results
with all of these experiences.

As you might have guessed, the couple's therapy didn't work
out so well. And the co-parenting therapy had similarly unpleas-
ant results. In fact, Elizabeth and I had the unique distinction
of having broken more than one therapist during our attempts
at co-parenting therapy. We are just that talented.

"Um, I think maybe you guys would be a better fit for another therapist. Let me not recommend anyone I actually know."

It turns out Elizabeth and I were just a better fit not trying
to fit together at all, in life or in a therapist's office.

The biggest obstacle that we faced in our attempts at
therapy was the fact that we were each really hoping (and

expecting) that the therapist would simply take our side in every disagreement. I think this happens a lot, where each member of a couple sees the therapist as a judge of sorts. We are each secretly hoping to present the case against our spouse, to which the therapist will respond, "I'm here to tell you, you are 100 percent in the right and your spouse is an asshole." It wouldn't hurt if there was a gavel involved as well, just to really bring it home.

Toward the end of our marriage and the beginning of our divorce, our communication had completely broken down to the point that all either of us said or heard were endless attacks on each other. We each agreed to go to a therapist at different points, not because we were really looking to heal, but because we were hoping this third party could talk some sense into our partner.

So, you know, starting off on really solid footing.

Our therapy sessions mostly consisted of more attacks, more blaming, and more screaming. And more than one therapist who looked utterly shell-shocked by our spectacle. You just know things are going well when your interactions with your spouse manage to unnerve professionals who literally sit around all day listening to couples argue about their problems.

After we split, I wanted desperately for us to figure out a healthy co-parenting relationship, but in the very beginning of our divorce it was clear that neither one of us was ready to figure out how to actually move forward. Every session seemed to be a competition to see who could fit as much of the past into the hour as possible. We were both exceedingly talented in this area.

I called off the co-parenting therapy, just like I'd called off the couple's therapy, because I didn't really need to pay $150 an hour to have someone listen to my ex and me yell at each other. We could do that shit for free.

After our failed co-parenting therapy, I sought out a therapist for just myself. I thought maybe working on myself might be the best way to get to a place where I could eventually work with Elizabeth again. But it was very clear very early on in my individual sessions that I didn't really have any interest in working on myself at all. I simply wanted this new therapist to listen to me bitch about my ex and assure me that of course I was right about everything.

Again, from a budgeting standpoint, this didn't seem like the best use of my money. I could call up my friends and bitch about Elizabeth for free.

And so I did.

I stopped going to therapy and leaned heavily into a few close friends. These friends knew me, they knew Elizabeth, and I didn't have to spend four sessions getting them caught up on my childhood. They knew all my shit, and they weren't scared to call me on it. And at that point, that was what I really needed.

Time went on, and the initial shock and awe of our divorce started to calm. I was doing well in life, and I was even in a new relationship. Clearly, I was cured, anyone could see that.

But I didn't like who I was in this new relationship. I didn't like how scared I was to be vulnerable, I didn't like how bad I was at communicating, I didn't like that I was so set in my ways. I didn't really like me. Not the me that I was because of my ex, or my kids, or my crappy marriage. Just me. I wanted to be better.

And that's when therapy started to work.

I was no longer interested in finding a therapist who would simply validate all of my grievances against my ex. I needed more than someone who would just tell me I was right. I knew I was wrong, and I knew it was time to be better.

I googled therapists in my area and tried a session with a few of them until I found one I really liked. (Please note: finding the right fit when searching for a therapist is so important. If it doesn't feel right, don't hesitate to keep looking.) Once I found a great therapist I booked a bunch of appointments and started digging in. How had I gotten to this point? What were the roots and the whys of how I moved through life and interacted with the people closest to my heart? Why were so few people ever allowed close? How could I do better the next time my heart was on the line?

Most of my work in therapy didn't have much to do with Elizabeth at all, because the roots of that failed relationship began growing well before she even came into my life. To figure out a way forward with her as a co-parent and figure out my life forward as a whole human, I had to go back to the roots. And I had to learn how to start growing something better.

Therapy is not for everyone, and only you know for sure if it would be a good fit for you. I firmly believe the biggest benefit of therapy is simply the opportunity to speak your story into the air, have someone else catch it for you, and turn it around so you might be able to see it from a new angle. Sometimes it can take trying a few different therapists before you find the one who can get you to engage with the process in a productive way.

The biggest requirement of any therapist, or any friend who is acting as your therapist, is that they are honest with you. You need someone who is supportive but stern, who doesn't judge but also doesn't tolerate your bullshit. (Also, it's worth noting that your friends are not actually therapists, and as such it is not actually their job to deal with your problems. If you find yourself calling the same friends over and over again, saying the same shit over and over again, it might be time to find an actual therapist. You need more help than your friends can give you over appetizers, and your friends deserve to have a happy hour that involves more than sad monologues.)

Wherever you are in your particular journey, therapy can usually provide at least a little direction and comfort. And trust me when I tell you that this particular journey is definitely going to be smoother if you have a trained professional guiding your scattered ass.

Here are some of the times throughout your divorce journey when therapy can make an appearance.

Therapy Before the End

(This is probably a moot suggestion if you picked up a book about divorce, but maybe it'll come in handy in your next partnership.) It's always a good idea to check in with a therapist before officially blowing up your marriage. Maybe there's something salvageable in your heap of burning garbage. Maybe an impartial third party can help you two communicate and get back on track. Maybe they can help you chip away at the walls you've built between the two of you.

Or maybe, if you're like me, you'll see a look of sheer terror in your therapist's eyes twenty minutes into your first session, and you'll know for certain it's time to officially end this shit show.

So either way, worth the $150.

Therapy at the Beginning of the End

I've known a few people who have successfully navigated co-parenting therapy soon after they split up with their spouse. I tend to think they are outliers, and most couples probably need a little cooling off period before attempting to do anything remotely collaborative. But maybe you and your ex will get it right straight out of the gate; it can't hurt to try.

Individual therapy around the time of your split can also be hit and miss. On the one hand, it's nice to have someone who is professionally obligated to listen to you sob/seethe about your ex ad nauseam, on the other hand, you might not quite be in the right headspace to actually get anything out of therapy just yet. But then again, maybe just having a safe place to unpack your angst might be worth the price of admission.

Therapy in the Middle

Who really knows where the middle is on a road that has no clear end point, but for me the middle felt like a noticeable shift from the ire of the beginning. I was no longer an open wound that was tender to every little thing. I was beginning to scab over a bit and could feel my blood pressure calming down from the steady red-zone pace it had maintained for months.

I was finally able to take a deep breath and see what was in front of me, instead of only focusing on the past. I could see a glimmer of a time when my scabs could become scars and this story of mine could be edited into something better.

When you get to this point, when you are ready to work on your future even if it means owning your own bullshit from the past, this is when the therapy can kick into high gear.

Therapy in the Middle of the Middle

I'm not sure if this applies to everyone, but after I spent several months deep diving in therapy, there came a point where I needed to come up for air. I needed to take a break from the diving and walk around on dry land for a little while, bringing along with me what I had been working on in therapy but not actively swimming around in the shit once a week.

In particular, I felt like my sessions were allowing me to spend too much time treading water in bullshit, injuries, guilt, and resentments of the past. I think that was important work to do, especially in the beginning, but something changed in me where I felt like it was time to start letting go, instead of hyper-focusing on unchangeable facts from ancient history (see Chapter 20, "Letting Go").

Therapy had helped me work through a lot of junk in my head, and taking a short break allowed me to participate in the present day with a clearer mind. I reengaged with my ex, ready to start building the new version of our relationship as co-parents. I started dating again, because I knew I was finally in a place to be of some value to another human. I moved around freely in the present, not having to dive into the past once a week with my therapist.

When I started back up with therapy, our focus shifted. We started talking about today and tomorrow, about the day-to-day work of moving through life, instead of only unpacking all the shit from the past. This might not be what works well for everyone, but for me, it was time to move forward, and I needed my therapy to move forward with me.

In all stages of therapy, if you are with the right therapist, there should be some fluidity to the work you are doing. There is not only one way to get where you are going, and sometimes the route winds around, takes side streets, retreats, and jumps ahead. Stay open to what feels right, and be gentle with yourself as you figure it all out.

Therapy at the End

Just kidding, there is no end. There's no graduating from therapy. (Although how much fun would it be to send those graduation announcements to friends and family? See Chapter 2, "Divorce Announcements Should be a Thing.") The work you do on yourself and for yourself in therapy is a forever sort of thing. But that doesn't necessarily mean you need to visit your shrink every week until the end of time.

Maybe you've talked and talked, you've done the work, you've made it to a place where you feel good about where you are, you've got some new tools packed, and you're hopeful about where you are headed. And maybe that's good enough for this stretch of highway. There's no shame in dropping your therapist off and going at it alone for the time being.

Just always remember that you are not actually "cured" simply because you feel like you've regained your footing after your divorce. And it doesn't mean you've somehow failed if you need some help at different times down the road. Therapy is always there, for a quick check-in or another deep dive.

Sometimes the best thing you can really hope for in regard to therapy is not getting to a point where you no longer need it but instead just getting to a point where you are able to identify simmering issues before they become life-altering explosions that wipe out everything in their vicinity. Being human is a lifelong, ever-evolving project and regular check-ins with a therapist are a great way to keep in touch with how your particular journey is progressing.

Isn't being a functioning adult so much fun?

DIVORCE SQUAD

Therapized

"Therapy was really helpful to me. I never realized how much of a codependent I was. I realize now that I did everything in my power to make his life easier, and it was my biggest stress. Now I can make decisions without thinking about how my husband will respond, it's so freeing. And I also learned that I always look for broken men who need repairing, so now I can see that as it's happening and stop it."

....

"We went to couple's therapy before we split up, and it was clear pretty early on that we weren't going to work, so we transitioned to co-parenting therapy right away. It was really helpful because we were building this next phase and communicating about it all along."

....

"She was always pushing me to go to therapy after we split up, because she thought a therapist would tell me she was right. She doesn't remember that I already went to therapy and discussed our issues. The feedback I got was that my wife's issues were likely traumatizing me and it's understandable for someone in my situation to retract and protect themselves by not reacting to every eruption. Of course, that is a one-sided perspective, but it did confirm that I'm not necessarily the 'crazy person' here, as she has tried to make me feel."

....

"The biggest thing I got out of therapy was learning how to avoid anyone that was anything like my ex in the future. There were reasons I was attracted to my ex, and I needed to fix those reasons so I could look for a relationship that was healthier for me."

....

"After a few years of being divorced we decided to go to a therapist and try to figure out a better way forward for our communication. We needed help in this area, and we were both willing to put some work into being better, for each other, and for our kids."

7

Who Gets Custody of the Friends

(how to navigate your friend circle after
you are no longer friends with your ex)

In the middle of our divorce drama, when the two of us were having an argument, Elizabeth threw out, "Well, your best friend agrees with me, she told me when I called her the other day to let her know how crazy you are being."

And that was the end of my relaxed attitude about shared friends, post-divorce.

When two people pair up, their lives tend to become inter-twined. Friends they each had before the relationship get mixed together with new friends they make as a couple. It's all one big happy friend fest . . . until it isn't. We talk a lot about how to split up property and kids and money after a divorce, but there are not a lot of set rules on how to properly distribute the friends.

In a perfect world a couple should theoretically be able to split up and not have it affect the friendships in their lives. They are just becoming two single humans; why would a change in relationship status have anything to do with friends? The answer, like everything else in this process, is complicated.

Each and every member of my Divorce Squad shared tales of friends picking sides post-divorce, even the divorcées who had drama-free splits. It seems as though friend allocation is just what happens after most marriages implode. You separate, you file for divorce, you work out a custody schedule for the kids, and then you find out what friends you get in the divorce settlement. It's like a rose ceremony to determine what group texts you still get to be part of.

During our journey toward separation, my ex would ask if I was comfortable with her staying friends with my friends after our split. At the time I said, of course, I had no problem with it at all. We had been together over a decade, and Elizabeth had established her own relationships with some of my closest friends. Why shouldn't she maintain those friendships after we broke up?

You know how that went.

For some, the friend distribution stung almost as much as their divorce. Heather, whose husband left her for another woman, told me, "It was this added layer of not being chosen. He chose another woman, then so many of our friends, because they were his friends from work, chose him. I was left without a spouse and without a community. Even my mom friends pulled away, because they just didn't want to have anything to do with our drama."

And I think that is where the answer lies. Most people just don't want to feel like they are in the middle of any drama, so they pick one side or the other, or they opt out altogether. It's shitty, but it's collateral damage that seems to happen in most divorces.

The easiest way forward on this particular issue is probably to evaluate your friendships and implement a yours/mine/ours labeling system. Don't reach out to your ex's friends, and don't do anything that puts mutual friends in an uncomfortable spot. Lean on the friends you know for sure are your solids, and give everyone else the space to determine where they want to land. Sides definitely need to be picked in some divorces, while others might evolve and relax enough that mutual friendships can survive without anyone feeling uncomfortable.

As our divorce got more contentious, I just didn't have the energy to play she said / she said with our mutual contacts, so I held on tight to my close friends and let everyone else fade away. And, to be frank, because my ex and I are such polar-opposite humans, there weren't a lot of people who wanted to remain friends with both of us. I actually think that might be the case in a lot of situations. Couples are a package deal, and once they split up, friends no longer have to hang out with the plus-one they weren't particularly fond of.

It's hard not to take the friend distribution personally, but in the end, or at least in the beginning, it's probably the easiest option for everyone. It's also a pretty blunt way to find out exactly where you stand with the different people in your life. Your friend circle may decrease in size during your divorce, but I argue that it will definitely grow in value.

After the dust settles, after you've pulled yourself out of the rubble, after you've rebuilt, the people who are still there, the people who never left, those are your people. Anyone else is no real loss, and ultimately they are one less Christmas card you have to send out. Think of all the cash you'll be saving on postage!

DIVORCE SQUAD

Odd Man Out

"Honestly, I wasn't interested in keeping any of our mutual friends. I wanted nothing that connected me to that old life."

....

"It was hard because once my wife left me most of our couple friends distanced themselves. They didn't stay friends with her either. It was like since I wasn't part of a couple they didn't know what to do with me or how to include me. Even the guys didn't seem like they were able to go do one-on-one stuff with me like we used to. It was weird and it definitely hurt."

....

"We worked in the same industry, so we had a lot of the same professional contacts that had become friends over the years. I left him, and it wasn't long before everyone knew it. I don't think he ever forgave me for making him look like a fool to all of those friends."

....

"He slept with his best friend's wife, so he basically lost me and all of his friends at the same time. His friends didn't know what happened right away, they only knew that he left me, so they rallied around him and ditched me. Then they found out the truth and all of a sudden their loyalties shifted. I didn't want anything to do with any of them though."

....

"My ex and I had a decent split, and neither one of us cared if we kept mutual friends. It was actually the friends who seemed to care. They would get awkward about spending time with us individually, like it wasn't allowed. They would speak in hushed voices to me about my ex. It was kind of funny, really. Eventually it all worked out, because they all finally realized it was okay to be friends with both of us—no picking sides needed."

8

Assembling Your Team

*(building your solid lineup to rally you
through your divorce)*

One of the most repeated pieces of advice I've heard from my
Divorce Squad is:

Do not send that text or email to your ex. Do not do it.

That advice will save you a lot of heartache in the early days,
because in the beginning of the end, when emotions are high,
you are going to be tempted to remain engaged with your ex to
make sure they completely understand every feeling you have
now or have had during your time together. Reflection and rage
are going to be in regular rotation, and you are going to feel the
need to share it all.

But look. It's over. It's been over. You guys didn't work. A text
or email is not going to change the years you spent together or
the turmoil in your gut now. So don't send the text or email to
your ex. And definitely don't dial their number. Just don't.

Instead, you need to assemble your support team and get
them ready to go several rounds with you during your divorce

journey. You will have texts and emotions that need to be set free and your friends are a much smarter direction to send them than your ex.

When thinking about what you are looking for in your support team, besides just people who will intercept your ill-advised emotional outburst to your ex, I need you to visualize the game show *Family Feud*. Two families line up on either side of the stage, with a member of each up at the buzzer podium, ready to give their answer. The host provides the prompt, "Name a fruit." One of the two contestants slams the buzzer and screams, with a huge smile on their face, "Rottweiler!"

After a pause—almost too long—their family standing behind them will clap like fools, "Good answer! Great job! It could be up there!"

I'm not sure if the family members are instructed by the producers to give enthusiastic support no matter what answer is given, but I am sure that those clapping family members are a really solid support system that could come in handy outside of a game show setting. In fact, this is exactly the sort of support system you're going to need post-divorce.

No matter what foolishness you participate in, no matter how many mental breakdowns you have, no matter what unfortunate hair styles you experiment with . . . you need people standing behind you clapping, "Good job! You got this! Who knows, maybe bangs *are* a good idea!"

In addition to general unwavering support and enthusiasm, your team of happy clappers is going to be very important in providing a buffer of sorts as you navigate your way through your divorce.

It's time to get that team together and get them clapping no matter what crazy comes out of you.

The A-Team

I was lucky because I had a pretty solid group of friends assembled pre-divorce, and I was able to call on a select few to form my support team when the shit hitteth the fan. I tried to be conscious of spreading out my irrational emotions so that I didn't overwhelm one or two people on too regular of a basis. In looking back at my team, the people who showed up over and over again, I think they all played a specific role in the lineup, and I recommend you look for people who can fill these roles in your life as well.

Your Ear

You're going to need at least one person who is willing to listen to your shit. I highly recommend finding more than one, because you are going to have a lot of shit that needs to be listened to. Your Ear is going to have to be available for both text and actual phone conversations. And in the very beginning, listening is going to be their primary function. They will occasionally throw out advice, but what you really need is simply an ear and a lot of "I know, I know." "You are totally right." "That IS some bullshit!" and "I think your new haircut looks fantastic."

My Ear was my friend Megan. I've known her for over a decade, and she was my Ear throughout my marriage as well. She knew the backstory, she'd been expecting this end for years, and she was ready to transition to this new portion of the program. The best thing about Megan is that she always seemed genuinely engaged in my mental breakdowns. She really cares, and I could feel her investment throughout our conversations.

In the beginning her ear was exactly what I needed: kind, encouraging, and supportive. As time went on, her ear evolved, because I needed to evolve. She started calling me on my shit more, cutting me off when I began to repeat the same tired story for the 875th time, and pushed me toward more productive conversations.

Which leads us to . . .

Your No Bullshit Bud

Eventually, and maybe immediately, you are also going to need someone who can get you to listen in return. The story you've created in your head about your marriage and your divorce is probably heavy on your ex being a complete piece of shit who deserves all the blame. And even if that's the truth (spoiler alert, it's not), you are still eventually going to have to look at yourself to figure out how you can build something better moving forward.

Your No Bullshit Bud gives zero shits about protecting your fragile ego. They are here to share the truth, and they aren't willing to entertain any bullshit you may be selling.

Damon was my go-to No Bullshit Bud. I would regularly call him up and say, "I need you to tell me if I'm being an asshole." And he would say, "I got you, hit me."

It wasn't that he would just call me an asshole and hang up; he'd call me an asshole and hammer out a way forward that might be little less ass-adjacent. He wasn't willing to treat me with kid gloves simply because I was emotional, but he was still in my corner, and he still understood that I was operating from a really raw place.

Find yourself a No Bullshit Bud, and get good at getting called out.

Your Conference Call

In football, special teams are the players who come out specifically for kickoffs and field goals and whatever else is special, I guess. The whistle blows and the special team comes on the field, does their one thing, then heads back to the sideline.

My special team was made up of three women I've known since we were all kids. When the going got tough, I would put in a request for a Conference Call, and the four of us would hash out the matter at hand. We'd meet over Zoom, sip wine, and figure out my life. I only needed these calls a couple times, but it was nice to have an entire committee available to discuss my problems.

If you have a group of friends and access to FaceTime, it's hard to beat a roundtable discussion when it comes to issue resolution. Alternatively, this meeting could happen in person, over apps and drinks, but there's something special about everyone in pajamas, slipping away from their kids, possibly Zooming from their closet with a bottle of wine. Keeping it all the way classy during your time of need.

Your In-Person People

Schedules and geography (and global pandemics) meant that most of my A-Team supported me via text or phone calls. But there were two people who got to see up close what a mess I was.

Michael and Jane were a couple who lived in my neighborhood. They had spent a lot of time with Elizabeth and me, all of our kids had grown up together over the years. Shortly after our split, Michael and Jane adopted me. Or at least it felt like they did. They invited me over for dinner or drinks, they arranged play dates with the kids, and Michael helped me with a bunch of house tasks that I had no idea how to do.

Talking and venting and sharing and crying (so much crying) is all very helpful and necessary following your divorce. But sometimes it's also nice to just sit with people and be human. To laugh and be normal, especially with the people who were a big part of your life pre-divorce.

If you have friends who live nearby, enlist them on to your team, and get together just like you did before your world exploded. The normalcy of it all will give you a glimpse of what life can and will look like once the dust settles.

Your Challenger

A couple of months after my divorce officially detonated, my agent texted me and said, "You know, you should write a book about this." I was on the couch, on a Friday night, eating a Snickers ice cream bar, watching depressing documentaries. I responded, "You know, I don't think I'm quite to the introspection portion of this program."

She wrote back, "That's why you should write."

I immediately brushed off her suggestion and frankly was a little annoyed by it. My agent is also my friend. She had become one of the people I texted during my divorce explosion, if only because as a book agent, she always enjoys a solid dramatic storyline. She wasn't randomly texting me during a horrible time, suggesting I monetize it. She was texting during a horrible time, challenging me to turn it into something better. I was annoyed because I was quite comfortable wallowing and wasn't ready to be productive just yet.

I dismissed her idea, and she took my no without pushing any further. But every time I'd share a new divorce development, she'd respond, "Write it!" And so I did (obviously).

Odds are, you aren't going to be writing a book about your divorce experience (although I do recommend destroying a few journals with your rage-writing). But it's always a good idea to surround yourself with people who are willing to push you past your current comfort level. The ones who tap you on the shoulder and say, "Hey, start walking this way. Even if you don't find exactly what you are looking for at least you are moving. It's time to start moving."

Listen to them, even if it takes you a minute to really hear what they are saying.

Your Action Team

The first summer of our split, both Elizabeth and I had two one-week stretches with the kids. These weeks allowed each of us the opportunity to take a couple extended vacations with the kids during their summer break. And these one-week stretches nearly killed me.

Up until that summer I had never been away from my kids for longer than three nights. And I could count on two fingers how many times I had even been away that long. In a decade. Seven nights away from my kids . . . was brutal.

The good news is, I knew it was going to be brutal, so I planned ahead. I have a group of friends that I met over twenty years ago while doing international volunteer work. Since we met, we have traveled all over the world together; they are truly some of my favorite humans. I reached out to this group and sent up a bat signal that I really, really needed a get-together during one of the weeks that I was going to be away from my kids. No questions asked, they were all in.

Six of us descended on a vacation spot, and our nonstop laughter did my heart good during a tremendously hard stretch of time. Most of this crew wasn't a part of my regular divorce communication rotation, but when I asked them to show up, they did.

Find the people in your life who are good at showing up for fun times. Put them in your pocket and call on them when you need an adventure to cleanse your soul.

••••

Your team may not look like mine, it may include more or fewer people, and some people may overlap into multiple categories. There are no rules to how you should build your team, but no matter what, you need to build one.

If you are like me, your instinct may be to internalize your issues and not bother anyone with your shit. You may want to put your head down, drink your wine, eat your ice cream, watch your depressing documentaries, and just try to ride this thing out on your own.

Don't do that.

Your friends care about you. They are probably worried about you and want to help. They may not know how to offer or how to reach out, but they are there, ready to listen to your shit. I promise that being vulnerable and open to support will serve you very well on the bumpy road ahead.

Reach out to a few friends with a simple text to break the ice, then ease into sharing your complete mental instability. I recommend starting these outreach efforts early and often, because divorce is not a challenge you want to take on without some happy clappers standing behind you, unwavering in their support no matter how ridiculous your actions are.

FUCK YOU, YOU FUCKING FUCK (A TIME FOR JOURNALING)
The Story

Shortly after I split from my ex, I became a bit obsessed with our story. Or more accurately, I became obsessed with her version of our story.

I told one of my friends, "She has created a completely different version of reality in her head."

My friend shrugged, "Yeah, that's sorta what happens in any relationship, isn't it?"

And that's when I stopped obsessing. Because duh. Of course we had two different versions of the story. That's how life works. Everyone's memory has a way of softening some corners and sharpening others.

You may be in a similar situation with your divorce. A situation where you feel like one of those NFL coaches running up and down the sideline, throwing their hands in the air, absolutely outraged by a horrible call made by one of the refs on the field. Maybe your ex is spreading an untrue version of your story, maybe they are gaslighting you when you confront them with the facts of the situation, maybe you can't believe what utter bullshit this person is telling themselves and anyone else who will listen.

I'm here to tell you that you cannot spend the rest of your life running up and down the sidelines trying to get your version of the story out to the world. Frankly, the world doesn't care. And eventually, you need to stop caring so much too.

But before you move on to healthy acceptance of the things you cannot change, let's first have our way with documenting the truth. For once and for all, get it out, get it on paper, let it free into the world. Spend a few pages in your journal telling your version of your story, whatever parts you feel need the most air time. Get it all out.

And then close the journal and leave the story there. Don't show anyone, don't tape it to your ex's forehead the next time you see them, don't transcribe it into a social media post for vindication. Just write it, read it, breathe it in and out. And leave it.

At a certain point you have to leave it somewhere, because it's an old story and you are busy creating something new, with a much better plotline. So, let's leave it here, today.

Rage it out. And let it go.

OUR STORY ... _____

_____

_____

_____

_____

_____

_____

_____

_____

9

Co-Parenting—Part 1

(you never want to see this person again and are tasked with completing the most important job on the planet with them—what could go wrong?)

Are you familiar with the reality show *The Amazing Race*? It's the one where teams race around the world, completing different challenges along the way. The teams are made up of two people with some sort of previous relationship: friends, spouses, coworkers, siblings, parent/child, and so on. They all start out the race full of smiles and high fives, and then inevitably a majority of the teams end up having some sort of spectacular meltdown while trying to decipher a map in rural Slovakia.

I believe that co-parenting after divorce is akin to the worst version of *The Amazing Race* ever.

Parenting (and *The Amazing Race*) is hard enough when the two team members start out copacetic. The gig gets considerably more difficult when it's already been determined (via a divorce filing) that the team is not super great at group projects (a.k.a. a functioning relationship).

But here's the thing. Co-parenting is the most important group project you are ever going to be a part of. And your final grade will be given by your child's therapist in roughly fifteen to twenty years, so you'd better take the assignment seriously.

The issue with this particular group project is that healthy co-parenting after divorce demands a level of maturity that is not easily accessible in the early days of a split. Divorces, whether they are civil or messy, all require a certain amount of healing. You have been wounded, and in the beginning of the end that wound is very open and raw. In time the injury slowly scabs over, and eventually it's just a scar that is always there but is no longer sensitive to touch.

The most challenging part of divorce with kids is that you are forced to do all that healing while having your wound repeatedly poked at by the person who caused the damage. This setup doesn't exactly lend itself to seamless rehabilitation.

Every therapist and book and podcast and blog will tell you that you simply need to put your head down and make co-parenting a peaceful endeavor because it is what is best for the kids and the kids are the #1 priority always. Of course we all know that. But sometimes it can be difficult to find peace in the middle of such an emotionally turbulent time. And even if you know that peaceful co-parenting is the destination, sometimes it can be unclear exactly how we are supposed to get there.

If you are having trouble finding peace but are really, really hoping it finds you someday, I've listed some things that helped me along the co-parenting path; perhaps some may help you as well. I've broken this subject up into two chapters (see also Chapter 18, "Co-Parenting—Part 2"), because it is by far the most difficult aspect of this whole experience, and it is the one that lingers as a general thorn in your side well after you've moved on from all the other hurdles of your divorce.

In this first co-parenting chapter, we are going to tackle some tips for the early days of your divorce, when things are still very raw but hold the key to determining how the rest of this project is going to go.

Be Honest with Your Kids, but Not Too Honest

When starting out on this project, be aware that your kids are the stars of the show. They are the reason we are all here, and they are the only reason we are all trying really hard not to screw this up. So don't keep them in the dark about what is going on. Be honest with your kids about the changes happening in your family. Their ages will determine how detailed you get, but if possible—and if this won't devolve into a he said / she said or blaming scenario—you and your ex should both sit down together with the kids and let them know that things will look different from here on out, but there is absolutely nothing changing about how their parents feel about them. Let them feel their feelings and ask their questions, but also don't expect everything to come out in one conversation.

A lot of times the feelings and questions will trickle out over time, as the reality of the situation starts to unfold. In those cases, the odds are you won't be sitting with your ex and will need to explain or comfort on your own. Whatever you do, no matter how volatile things are in your divorce, use all your internal fortitude to stay neutral and respectful toward your ex when answering any questions. Be honest with the kids, but only as honest as a kid brain can really process.

Speaking kindly—and if that is a problem, at the very least, neutrally—about your ex to your kids will be an exercise in restraint and maturity. Go ahead and get real comfortable with restraint and maturity, they are going to be called upon quite a bit during the rest of your co-parenting adventures.

Get Started Early and Often on the Worst Group Project Ever

I'm not sure this really could have been avoided, but I think the single biggest mistake my ex and I made on our journey was that we did not immediately establish our new co-parenting relationship right after our split. Our initial split was amicable, a little too amicable. Other than the fact that I moved out, things didn't change very much with our family unit. We were still way too intertwined in each other's lives, and we were making no efforts whatsoever to figure out how things would realistically look moving forward as two independent people.

This strategy helped soften the blow of the initial split, but it made things very challenging when my ex brought a new partner into the mix a few months after I left. We had failed to adequately set up the boundaries and dynamics of our co-parenting relationship by the time my ex partnered up again, and that failure cost us months and months of hiccups as we stumbled through figuring out how to do this project together, while apart, with a new person involved in what should have been a two-person conversation.

Other couples are not able to settle quickly into a peaceful co-parenting relationship for a myriad of reasons, including abuse, utter betrayal, extreme disgust, and combative communication. Sometimes even speaking to each other feels impossible, so peaceful collaboration is not quite on the list of options. And I get it. Sometimes taking a minute to cool off will give you the biggest chance at long-term success with this project.

But I'm here to tell you that you are eventually going to have to figure something out, and it's in your best interest to figure it out before either one of you partners up again. And trust me when I tell you that one or both of you will partner up much sooner than you are expecting. No one besides the two of you should be involved in determining what your co-parenting relationship is going to look like, so the sooner you can start the process, the easier it will be to establish ground rules before other people come on the scene.

Get Back to the Table

When you choose divorce, you are effectively giving up on any hope that you and your spouse can make it work. The complete abandonment of optimism can actually be liberating, because odds are you had been trying to force it to work for quite some time before your split. In choosing divorce, you are acknowledging that your relationship is all the way DONE and the two of you JUST DON'T WORK. You can *finally* rejoice in being free. End of story.

But. Turns out the story is not quite over. Sonofabitch.

In my case I had seen divorce as an out, but co-parenting pulled me back in. Like the mob but with more cussing.

My ex's favorite description of the two of us has always been, "We speak two different languages." She's always meant it as a throwing-her-hands-up-in-the-air-why-bother-it'll-never-work-we-will-never-understand-each-other sort of statement.

But one day, as I was sitting around a table with the ex and her new girlfriend, the new girlfriend cut the ex off and said sharply, "But people learn new languages all the time, so that's not a valid excuse."

And that's what we had to do.

The two of us. Two polar opposite humans who speak different languages. Who gave up on each other and on partnership years and years ago. We had to come back to the table and learn a new language. Specifically, we had to learn each other's language. All that disconnection and avoiding that I had done for years? It was no longer an option. All her throwing her hands up in the air and proclaiming us unable to understand each other? Also not going to work.

We were going to have to put our energy and inclination into figuring out how to meet each other somewhere in the middle, somewhere we hadn't been for years.

Start from Today

Once you've gotten back to the table and are ready and willing to do this thing with this person, the biggest piece of advice I can give you is to start from today. Today is the first day of your new relationship. You are no longer married, you are no longer partners, you no longer have to do life together. So all the days that came before, when you were married and doing life together, are moot. They don't matter to this new relationship.

They can't matter, or this project is going to go off course every thirteen minutes.

In the beginning this is going to be very difficult. Your past is still wrapped around your heart, and it's still a very open wound that you are dealing with every day, so it's going to be nearly impossible to separate it from the present. But trust me when I tell you that eventually it has to be separated.

There may be a time when the two of you are ready to hash out your years together and engage in healthy discourse that honors both of your experiences. That time is not now. That time is thousands of dollars of therapy down the road.

Right now the two of you need to start setting up the foundation of what is going to become your new relationship. This sounds very hippie-dippie and almost naive, but I think it is important. The last version of your relationship didn't work out so well, so there's no reason to use it as a blueprint for this new venture.

You are no longer partners, so things can look a bit different; boundaries and rules can be more defined. This can take a little time to get right. In the beginning of my new co-parenting relationship, my ex would constantly call me "reactionary." I believe she meant this as an insult. Each time she would do something that was inconsiderate or selfish I would respond by doing something equally inconsiderate and selfish. I'd spent twelve years not reacting to her shenanigans, so I was no longer willing to let them slide. On her side, every time she thought I was being too controlling, she'd push back, hard, and would refuse to go along with what I was saying. She'd spent twelve years feeling controlled and was no longer willing to let it slide.

We'd both push way too hard trying to make our point and set our new boundaries, but eventually the other one got the message, and we were forced to figure out new ways of doing things to avoid explosions every thirteen minutes. This meant starting from today over and over and over again.

I think it's also worth noting that this has been by far the biggest hurdle in our co-parenting efforts post-divorce. No matter how many steps forward we take, it seems there is always the potential for the past to rear its head into the present. When this happens, we are instantly knocked off solid footing and thrown back into old attacks and defenses. And then eventually, after the dust has settled, we have to reset and start from today, again. And again. All this is to say, none of this co-parenting stuff just magically clicks and goes smoothly for the rest of time. It's constant, tedious, sometimes volatile work.

Show up for it anyway.

Set Yourself Up for Success

A big part of your success is going to rely on figuring out work-arounds to avoid blowups. Be realistic about what each of you is capable of and what each of you needs in order to keep this ship from capsizing.

First of all, I highly recommend having two sets of everything, so that the kids can simply exist at each house without requiring a ton of item swaps to take place. This may seem elementary, but kid exchanges and navigating two houses is difficult enough without also having to make sure the kids have an entire bag packed with all of their necessities each time. There will always be something left behind, and that is going to lead to unnecessary communication and frustration.

I've read books that recommend the opposite of this strategy, with the argument that two of everything makes the kids feel split in two. But I argue that packing up a whole life to move from house to house makes kids feel like they are merely visiting each location. Having two completely set up homes provides the kids with comfort and consistency and roots. They aren't guests staying for a while; this is their home.

When soccer season started for our kids, we had one uniform for each of them, with the agreement that the uniforms would be switched back and forth between the parents during the week for the next weekend's game. This plan lasted one week. On Week 2 Elizabeth didn't get me the uniforms back before she headed out of town. There was back-and-forth, arguing, pulling my hair out, and uniform delivery by a random helper an hour before the games started.

The next day I bought a second set of uniforms so that we each had a set at our house. We tried to do the back-and-forth and it didn't work—I wasn't interested in testing it again. One of the biggest lessons of my marriage and divorce has been, "Believe it when something tells you it's broken." Let's repeat it so you can highlight it twice: *believe it when something tells you it's broken.*

This uniform strategy can be applied to a lot of different issues that arise when trying to successfully co-parent. If something is telling you it's not working, believe it and adjust accordingly. Don't try, try again. Accept and adjust. Adjust the plan, adjust your expectations, adjust your reaction. Your old way of doing things together led to a divorce, maybe it's time to explore things from a different perspective in order to get different results.

You Can Hit Pause

In the early days/weeks/months, no matter how much you log-ically know that you have to do this project with this person, there will be times when the emotions of the thing will make it nearly impossible to pull off. Maybe you are going through a rough patch on your own, maybe you two are butting heads, maybe your behavior toward each other is falling back into un-healthy routines or disrespect. When this happens, when the situation feels like it's going off the rails, it's okay to take a pause on the project. Of course, there is not a pause available for the actual parenting, but there are ways to take a step back from your interactions with the ex.

When my divorce was new, my ex and I would fall too easily into arguments over text. The simplest of conversations would deteriorate into name calling and the unearthing of twelve years' worth of resentments. There was absolutely nothing positive that could come from those arguments once we both dug in our heels for a battle. So, on several occasions I simply blocked my ex in my phone for weeks at a time. If she wanted to get ahold of me, she could email anything that needed to be addressed. My emails went to the same phone, and I checked them frequently, so there was little to no delay in receiving necessary messages.

Removing that constant intrusion via text allowed me the chance to regroup and reset, so that I could reengage with her after a little time had passed.

There are also several apps (search "co-parenting" in the app store) that allow you to put boundaries on the level of com-munication between the two of you. They organize custody schedules and provide a very businesslike way to communicate about very nonbusiness matters. Some have tone meters that can basically proofread any and all communications for hysteria and keep your interactions civil. They also offer the option of setting limits on the number of texts that can be sent in a day or what time the texts can be sent. All of this can prove to be very helpful during those times when hostile communication threatens to throw your whole project off track.

Remember, You Have to Do This

This seems like a pretty obvious statement, but it's one that you are going to need to repeat to yourself many, many times over the years. Because many, many times over the years you will really, really want to not do this project with this person.

In the early days your frustration with this situation may leave you seething on a pretty regular basis. You'll want to give up. But I'm so sorry to tell you, that is not an option. You have to do this.

Go into the closet, scream at the top of your lungs, and then head back to the co-parenting table with your ex. This group project is a long-term one, so get settled in for the ride. Your kids are counting on you.

DIVORCE SQUAD

Co-Parenting Ups and Downs

"I treat it like a business relationship. Approaching it that way removed the emotion from everything but my daughter. Conversations about our daughter would take a detour and I would have to circle back to what the reason for the meeting was. Literally side-stepping passive aggressive or personal comments just to get back to the reason we were communicating in the first place."

....

"I hate when people say to treat it like a business relationship. We are not in business! We are raising kids together! I have a text string going with your mom, is that a business relationship? No. I always thought it was so insulting to our time together and to our kids to call it a business relationship."

....

"My in-laws were the main reason we weren't able to co-parent well. They hated me because I left him, so my ex had to hate me too. I really believe that if it weren't for the people in his life, we could have done a much better job co-parenting together. He just never agreed that our kid was more important than his family's opinion of me."

....

"Eventually I just started texting his girlfriend directly because she was more responsive than my ex-husband. It's a weird thing to be co-parenting with someone who is not the actual parent, but it's just the way things happened."

....

"We're both pretty levelheaded and reasonable people, so that helps. We also have very similar parenting styles. We have a joint calendar that we use to keep all the kids' activities and our parenting schedule on. I'd say open and honest communication is the most important thing. We do most of our communicating in person. We are both pretty flexible when it comes to schedule changes and helping each other out. I'm proud of how well we are doing for our kids, and for each other."

10

Single Parenting

(the race to become the "fun" parent)

We've all heard the phrase "Disneyland Dad": you know, the dad who is big on spoiling their kid with trips and toys to make up for his lack of involvement in actual parenting duties. I think we all become a little bit of a Disneyland Parent right after divorce, but not because we are checking out of parenting; instead, we are trying EXTRA HARD to compensate during such a tumultuous time. Also, our marriage has been broken into two teams, and we are desperate for our kids to pick us as the fan favorite.

This, of course, is ridiculous, but it is very on brand for the absurdity of divorce.

The first summer after our split, Elizabeth and I each had the kids for two one-week blocks of time. Pre-divorce we would usually take the kids on one summer vacation out of town. We'd rent an Airbnb near a beach and spend five days or so chasing the waves with the kids. We all enjoyed the ocean, but our children are homebodies who are happiest when they are in their own space, so they were always excited to get back home after a vacation away.

Completely ignoring this fact about our kids, Elizabeth and I both planned vacations for each of the weeks that we had the kids during the summer. This meant that these two homebodies were away from home for four weeks out of their two-month summer break. They went to three lakes, an ocean, the mountains, a Lego amusement park, the Jelly Belly factory, a safari adventure, fishing, hiking, and jet skiing. Toward the end of the summer, my son, who is not a fan of school, exclaimed to the heavens, "I can't wait for school to start so we can stop GOING SO MANY PLAAAAACESSSS."

50 Percent On

Elizabeth and I are both really good, involved parents. There is absolutely no reason why either one of us needs to pull out Disneyland antics to overcompensate. But that didn't stop either of us from giving it our all to win our kids' affections in the beginning. I was planning trips, and crafts, and activities, and playdates with abandon. Looking back on that time, I can see that what I was actually doing was trying to dance around how sad I was. I didn't want to slow down long enough for them to sense my pain, so I was distracting all of us with the shiny objects of fun and adventure.

Eventually, I started to agree with my son's assessment of the situation. It was all just too exhausting. As I got more comfortable in my post-divorce life and found happiness again, I no longer needed the shiny objects. And that's when the real fun began; that's when the three of us started to chill together.

As I mentioned, my kids are homebodies. They love to spend a day lounging around the house, creating elaborate scenes with their toys, playing video games, running around in the backyard, or curled up on the couch reading. So, instead of planning activities and outings and Forced Family Fun, I just started letting them take the lead. I started saying yes.

I'd craft with them, let them read me their books, pushed them on the swings in the backyard, or looked up recipes to whatever random dessert they wanted to try making. We'd sit for hours snuggling on the couch, talking about animals and video games and bad puns. We decorated the house with abandon for every holiday because nothing made my daughter happier. They helped out with the cooking and cleaning because they knew I was managing our house alone and they wanted to contribute. We had dance parties, made up songs, and went on bike rides around the neighborhood. I finally had the energy to say yes to whatever delights of childhood they wanted to engage in.

All of that was where the gold of this situation was found. Yes, it profoundly sucked that I only had my kids half the time, but oh my goodness was I a damn good mom during that half. Why? Because I had a break every couple of days to rejuvenate! By the time I got them back, I was well rested and ready to say yes.

When I used to have them full time, I was always exhausted. Granted, a lot of that had to do with the fact that they were much younger back then and inherently more exhausting creatures. But the day-to-day of kids and career and a failing marriage left me wiped out most days. I would say no to the kids most of the time because I just couldn't summon the energy necessary for anything more than minimum requirements.

The other day I was rubbing my eyes at the dinner table, because my allergies were acting up. My daughter said, "Are you tired, Mommy?" I told her no, my eyes were puffy from being outside earlier. And then I flashed back to our dinners when

Elizabeth and I were still together. Pretty much every night I would spend at least part of the meal with my head in my hands, rubbing my face, from exhaustion or from frustration with whatever disagreement Elizabeth and I were having during dinner. "Tired" was just a constant physical and emotional state for me. For years.

The other night, when I rubbed my eyes, my daughter flashed back to those times and wondered if I was tired again. It made me stop and think, and I realized I haven't been exhausted in a really, really long time. Life is not heavy anymore. Our house is not running on empty, and all of us can feel the difference.

50 Percent Off

The other, more difficult, part of parenting after divorce is the amount of time you spend not parenting. It's hard to adequately describe how unnatural it feels to go from being with your kids every single day of their existence to spending days on end without seeing them.

Losing any of your time with your kids has a bit of an empty nest vibe to it. You drop them off at their other house and drive away. They have a whole life that you are not a part of. This is not how things are supposed to go, this is not supposed to be happening yet. Your heart has not had time to prepare for that drive away from them.

No matter how much time passes, I'm not sure I'll ever get used to the fact that my kids are living half their lives without me. They come home from my ex's house and tell me about things they've done, and it stabs me in the heart every single time. That stabbing feeling is not jealousy, it's not rage. It's grief.

It's the grief of having grown these two humans from scratch, with the intention of being there for their first eighteen years, only to lose half of their childhoods because I couldn't make my marriage work.

I know how lucky I am that my kids have two safe, loving homes, I know that in my core. They are happy children and that makes me a happy mom. But I also know in my core that I will never stop grieving the time I've lost with them, especially as they get older and their childhoods become more and more finite.

But the biggest dichotomy of this whole situation is how much of my newfound happiness has been discovered during my time away from the kids. It feels wrong to even type that, to even acknowledge how amazing it can be to have half of your life available to rediscover living.

It's hard to reconcile all the conflicting emotions of parenting after divorce. The guilt of breaking up a family unit, the elation of being free of an unhappy household. The joy of becoming a better parent for your kids, the heartbreak of not having them with you 100 percent of the time. The frustration of having to create a whole new version of life, the excitement of *getting* to create a whole new version of life. The confusion of not knowing which one of these emotions is true, and the mess of having to acknowledge that they all are.

It's okay if you feel like you are in a never-ending game of Whac-A-Mole when trying to deal with all these different emotions every time they pop up. In the beginning it may feel like all you are doing is whacking away at feelings while simultaneously trying to protect your kids from all of them.

Unfortunately, there is little you can do about all of these emotions, besides acknowledging them, feeling them, and trying to keep them from knocking you off your feet every second of your life. In the early days of divorce, this can mean a lot of Disneyland Dad antics when you have the kids and a lot of crying on the couch when you don't. All of that is okay, and none of it is permanent, I promise.

When you are ready to explore options outside of sobbing into decorative pillows, head over to the next chapter, where I dive into more productive ways to fill your (very quiet) child-free time. There's an opportunity waiting for you, when you are ready, to turn this new reality into something so much better for yourself and your kids.

DIVORCE SQUAD

Part-Time Parent

"It's a weird thing to say, but I feel like I got to know my kids so much better when it was just the three of us without my ex. There was no one to distract me from them, and we started having so much fun together. I've never introduced them to anyone I've dated, because I didn't want to share my time with them. Even when I have a friend over every once in a while for dinner or something, I don't like that this adult is taking up my time, I'd rather be hanging out with them. We have a really cool bond that I don't think would have ever happened if I'd stayed married."

....

"The logistics of parenting without my ex-husband were difficult because my job doesn't have normal hours. I had to rely on him a lot and our schedule had to be flexible. My mom helped me a lot, and I ended up hiring a part-time nanny because I really needed to feel like I was covering my half of the time without having to ask him for help."

....

"My ex definitely stepped up eventually and became a better dad by far after the divorce. I actually believe if we would've stayed together, he wouldn't be the dad he is now. He had them 50 percent of the time and had to step up. Also, he knew everyone expected him to fail and he has too much pride to fail, so he was kind of forced into being a good dad."

....

"I tried to concentrate on just being happy when the kids were with me. We had all been so unhappy before the divorce, our house had been so unhappy all the time. It was nice to start over and have a house where things, even though they were hard, were happy again."

11

All the Time in the World

*(how to fill the [very quiet] time
you aren't with your kids)*

Kids are loud. Happy kids, sad kids, playing kids, kids watching the blaring TV. They are all LOUD. It's sorta their thing. That loudness just becomes part of your life once you have kids, you barely even notice it after a while. But then you get divorced, and you lose part of your time with your kids. And your house . . . it gets really fucking quiet. It sorta feels like an isolation booth. A silent, claustrophobic space, with the whole world happening outside.

It wasn't until I moved back into our family home that the silence completely knocked me over.

I had never really been in that house without them; they had lived, pooped, laughed, played, peed, cried, eaten, puked, danced, and destroyed every square inch of that space. It was theirs. So, when I moved back into that house and had to be there half the time without the kids . . . I wasn't sure how to even exist in the space without them there. It felt bizarre. And. So. Fucking. Quiet.

The quiet was more than just an absence of sound, it was an absence of life. It was an absence of the life that used to exist in that house, the one that included me being with my kids every single day. The reality of that absence hurt like hell.

I wasn't quite sure what to do with this hurt. My instinct was to get out of the house, to make plans, to fill the silence with anything and everything I could. But I didn't do that.

Instead, I sat down on the couch and I forced myself to really feel what I had done. I had done this. I had ended my marriage, I had split up my family, I had caused this silence. And I needed to fully accept that this was what my home was going to feel like from now on. It—and I—were going to feel very empty 50 percent of the time.

I'd been avoiding these feelings for months (see Chapter 5, "The Seven Stages of Divorce") and it was finally time to accept them (see Chapter 5, "The Seven Stages of Divorce"). I cried. A lot. I talked to the animals. A lot. I attached my ass to my couch and read books or played games on my phone. I rolled all around in the silence and made it familiar.

And then, once my heart stopped breaking every time the kids left my house, I started exploring the upside of this new arrangement. And oh, what an upside there was to be found.

Look, we all love our kids. That goes without saying. But if we are being honest, they are a bit of an energy suck. Raising kids day in and day out can get exhausting. In the hustle and bustle of kids and life and work and partners, most of our days feel like a never-ending to-do list that never gets close to to-done.

But you know what can make all that easier? If you suddenly have half of your time free to kick the shit out of your to-do list!

I work from home and only have my kids half the week. This leaves me A LOT of time to myself. Once I stopped being sad about all this solitude, I opened my mind to the upside. I started delighting in my productivity. If there was a project I wanted to do around the house . . . I just did the project. I was on top of the laundry, presents were purchased well in advance of birthdays and holidays, my house was clean, the oil in my car was changed on time. I was adulting like a motherfucker.

I was also able to dabble in the "self-care" that social media is constantly telling moms they need to do, even though most moms don't even have time to shut the door to the bathroom, let alone take a relaxing bubble bath.

But guess what? I had all the time in the world!

So I worked out, slept in, had dinner with friends, climbed mountains, and made out with quite a few people (Please see Chapter 22, "New You"). And let me tell you something, Instagram was right! All that shit was a lot of fun.

Then after having all that fun, I'd get my kids back and be rejuvenated for them. I was no longer exhausted twenty-four hours a day, and I was no longer in an unhappy marriage, so I was no longer a shell of a human. I was present for the kids, I was excited to be with them, and I wanted to maximize the time we had together.

It didn't magically stop hurting that I don't get to tuck them in every night and wake up with them every morning. That I'm not always able to be the one who comforts them when they are sick. That I spend half of the holidays without my kids. I'm not sure any of that will ever stop hurting.

But that doesn't mean I can't acknowledge and take advantage of the upside, even if it took me quite a while to open my mind up to the possibility of a silver lining.

When you are ready to lean into your upside, I have a few recommendations for how to pass the time.

Lean Into the New Normal

Adult Fun

Parenthood, especially new parenthood, is decidedly light on good times. Life tends to come to a bit of a standstill, and your criteria for a fun night consists solely of child(ren) going to and staying asleep.

But now you have some of your nights free! Good times await!

Try to think back to the things you used to do for fun before you had kids. Now make a point to go do those things. Make dinner plans with friends, go catch a drink after work with a colleague, make out with a stranger in a bathroom. You know, *adult* things.

Adult Shit

Unfortunately, just because you don't have your kids all the time doesn't mean your other adult responsibilities are also on a shared custody schedule. There are still bills to pay, laundry to fold, groceries to buy, and surfaces to vacuum. But all of those chores can be done a little bit easier if you don't have kids running around bouncing My Little Ponies off your head.

Meetup Groups

Most of your friends have super-full lives and aren't always free to entertain you. And making new friends is not something that is easily done after a certain age.

Meetup is an app that has a variety of groups organized around a variety of interests. There are book clubs, hiking groups, trivia nights, bunco, foodies, and more. Scour the app, look for a group that interests you, and force yourself to go to one of the in-person or virtual meetups. Human interaction is fun! I promise.

Work Out

I put this on here because we all have visions of being the kind of person who would of course start working out, if only we had the time.

Welp, you have the time. So maybe you could work out? Make sure you really explore all the other things on this list first, though, just to be safe.

Basket Weaving

Remember that hobby you started that one time? That thing that seemed sort of fun but ultimately ended up buried in your closet somewhere? It's time to revisit that hobby.

Pull out the craft supplies, dust off that tennis racket, pick up where you left off on your great American novel. Do the thing. It's time.

Absolutely Nothing

Alternatively, I fully support you doing absolutely fucking nothing. Doing the things is overrated, and you've been through a lot. Divorce is hard. Parenting is hard. Life is hard. Take your alone time to be still and do absolutely nothing.

Don't make anyone dinner, don't answer anyone's email, don't even think about cleaning that cat box. Sit down. Put your feet up. And do nothing. You've earned it.

DIVORCE SQUAD

Silent Nights

"At first, I couldn't be home alone. He would pick up the kids and I had to leave the house. I went to my friend's all the time and drank wine on her couch. I HATED being alone. I also shut the doors to my kids' room, to pretend like they were in there sleeping."

....

"I didn't clean up my kids' toys when they were gone. Somehow it made it feel like they were still in the house if their messes were still there."

....

"I felt guilty about not feeling guilty about them not being with me all the time."

....

"I wandered the aisles of Target . . . "

....

"Before the divorce life was always so busy, always different things going on. School stuff, sports, friends, scouts. After we split up and the kids were gone half the time and the quiet in the house almost killed me. It was awful. There were so many new things I had to do when my wife and I split up, so I tried to do those things when I didn't have the kids. I would grocery shop, do laundry, clean the house. Anything to keep myself busy and not think about how quiet it was."

....

"It's weird to say, but I really feel like I found myself again after divorce. I'd spent so many years managing everything in my house, to the point where I would be completely wiped at the end of every day, with not even a second for myself. And now, I have so much time for me again. I miss my kids, yes, but I also really love the person I've found in myself in my time without them."

12

Your Replacement

(adding new partners to the equation)

Relationships are an equation. Adding kids changes the equation, separating the parents alters the equation again. And when new partners come into the mix, they can really fuck with the math. Some of them delight in causing a disruption, others do their best to remain out of the fray. But no matter who they are or what they do, they are now part of the equation. Results may vary.

Imagine, if you will, a game show of sorts. You're at the beginning of a divorce, and you are brought on stage. Over to the left a spotlight blasts on, revealing a woman. She's a complete stranger.

The host points to her and exclaims:

"Congratulations! This is the new co-parent of your children!"

"Wait, what?"

"She has some really helpful notes to share with you on how you should parent. And also, as an added bonus, she will now be intricately involved in your divorce proceedings, using all the facts provided to her by your ex!"

"Wait, can I talk to her?"

"I'm sorry no, maybe in a year or so."

"I don't get to speak to the complete stranger cohabitating with my kids?"

"No, I'm sorry, stop asking! But as a lovely parting gift, you don't have to do life with your ex anymore."

"We'll, that's something, I guess."

And so is the joy of your ex partnering up after a split.

But also imagine, if you will, another game show. You are brought up on a stage and Door #1 opens to reveal the person you just started dating. Aw, you really like them, you think there could be a future with them.

But wait, there's more.

"Behind Door #2 are two children that are not yours, but you will have to care for and love if you decide to stay with Door #1 Person. If things don't work out? You lose both doors."

"Oh, okay, well, that's a little scary. But, okay, I'm willing to do that. As long as—"

"And then! Behind Door #3 is a complete stranger who will be annoyingly involved in your life for the next decade or so. And they don't like you."

"Wait, what?"

"The two adults behind Doors #1 and #3 really don't like each other, but they both love the kids behind Door #2 and will spend the next decade pushing and pulling and cycling between rage and grace in an effort to do right by Door #2, while also trying to limit the level of bullshit they are willing to tolerate from each other. You get to be a bystander to this clusterfuck, and also you will need to put the kids first, your needs second, while accepting that ultimately the other adults call the shots, not you."

"Wait, what?"

And so is the joy of partnering up with a divorced parent. It is really a load of fun for everyone involved.

I've spent a long time trying to wrap my mind around how I responded to my ex partnering up so soon after our split (see Chapter 3, "Blowing Things Up"). I haven't been looking for excuses so much as whys. Because my reaction really made no sense on a logical level.

When this new woman came on the scene, she cared about my ex, was nice to my kids, and finally freed me from the last ties I had to my broken relationship. She was, quite frankly, the absolute best thing that could have happened to all of us.

And yet.

She still annoyed the hell out of me.

At the time I chalked up my vitriol to pure pettiness, but I think the whys have deeper roots than that (although pettiness was still a very large part of the mix, for sure).

Let's look at the math: I moved out in June. In mid-October Elizabeth was still telling me how she was lonely and missed having someone to talk to. By the middle of November, she proclaimed that she had met someone and was in love. Six days later we sat the kids down to let them know that we would be doing things a lot more separately moving forward; I wasn't going to be at the family home every day like I had been since the split. Five days after that chat, the new girlfriend was in my old home, setting up Christmas decorations with my kids, followed by a sleepover that night.

Lesbians move at speeds that are not commonly found in nature. And these two were the most lesbian lesbians who have ever lesbianed. (Although, in chats with my Divorce Squad, apparently everyone is a little lesbian after a divorce, with rapid partnering up being a pretty regular occurrence.)

Something about someone in my home, playing house with my kids, five days after we told them our dynamics were changing, snapped my brain in a way that made no sense to me or anyone who knew me as a relatively unflappable person.

I saw a quote the other day that read, "I sat with my anger long enough, until she told me her real name was grief." And now that I have a bit of distance from the brain snapping, I can clearly see that all my emotions regarding this new woman were firmly rooted in the overwhelming grief I felt from having lost half of my time with my children.

A couple of days after I found out about the new girlfriend, I broke down in tears with the kids. It was official. I was going to lose 50 percent of my time with them. I'd spent years avoiding this, staying in an unhappy relationship because I just couldn't bear the thought of losing them, and now it was happening. But how do you truly process the grief of losing your kids? First step: get really fucking angry.

Was it this new girlfriend's fault that I left my marriage and lost 50 percent of my time with the kids? No. But her arrival was when I lost 50 percent of that time. And I was deeply jealous that as I was losing my seven- and nine-year-olds, she was gaining them, these amazing little humans she had no hand in building.

And the kids loved her. She was texting them, calling them, making them gifts, bringing crafts to do together. She was Mary fucking Poppins.

My friends, who could tell that this woman was irritating the hell out of me, would repeatedly ask, "What were you expecting exactly? You left. Of course Elizabeth would get a new partner right away."

Of course she would. And what more could I ask for besides someone who cared about my ex and was nice to my kids? There was nothing more I could ask for. And yet there was nothing I could do to control my extreme dislike of this woman. It was almost primal, the anger in my gut when I thought of a stranger creating a bond with my children.

When I called out my pettiness to one of my Divorce Squad, she countered with, "But you know what? Is it petty? Because being a mom is a big, no joke, big fucking deal. And the way that you mother, the second that you have the ability to think about a future, you're thinking about how you are going to mother. You spend all this time, you've made these little people *in your body*, you're doing your absolute best, you're doing everything for these kids. And then all of a sudden—BOOM— the relationship ends, which doesn't change your mothering at all. And then somebody else comes in, and they're taking parts of your role. And the one thing that I never thought I would have to feel anxious or jealous about—I never thought motherhood would be a role of comparison. I wasn't prepared to have to think about that. So yeah, I'm sure it's petty. But these kids are mine! I made these! You don't get to come and sign the artwork after I created it!"

When I look deeper at that sentiment from my divorced friend, it is clear what she is actually talking about: vulnerability. Children are the one relationship in life where it feels 100 percent safe to give every ounce of yourself. They are yours and you are theirs. And if you aren't a complete asshole, that bond will never be broken.

But after a divorce, when you lose part of your time with your kids, when other people begin entering their lives, when those people have opinions about your parenting, you can begin to feel vulnerable. You begin to question whether other people can break that unquestionable bond. Of course this is a ridiculous emotion, but sound logic is in short supply during this time, and vulnerability can very easily turn into insecurity and pettiness and jealousy.

But on the flip side of my pettiness and grief is the new girlfriend whose only mistake was choosing to get involved with a person who came with an entourage. She went all in with someone who wasn't quite all out of her entanglements with a previous life, and there was a steep learning curve for all of us.

She was doing her best in dealing with a new relationship, new kids, and her new girlfriend's seemingly unstable ex. While I was doing my absolute worst in processing what it meant to finally be out of an unhealthy relationship while simultaneously losing my children as a result. It was not my best look.

One day, in the middle of trying to move toward a more friendly co-parenting relationship, Elizabeth said to me about her girlfriend, "Do you remember how my cousins used to make you feel? Don't make her feel like that."

I was so confused by her mentioning this, because I had no idea where she was going with the comparison. Elizabeth's cousins had a big family, five siblings, each with a spouse and kids. They were very tight knit, and anytime we were around them I felt like an outsider who didn't belong in their clique. It took me a minute to process what Elizabeth was saying by comparing me to her cousins. She was saying that her girlfriend felt like the odd man out. I was baffled.

How on earth could she feel like the odd man out, when I was *literally* the odd man out of the house and shiny insta-family the two of them were creating with the kids?

"Because you are the mom, Dawn. You'll always be the mom. The four of us, you, me, and the kids will always be a family. Of course she feels like she's on the outside of that."

I was dumbfounded. But I listened. And it changed my posture about the whole situation. This woman wasn't working so hard to impress my kids because she wanted to replace me; she was working so hard because she was trying to find a place in this family that had been formed twelve years before she arrived. And how daunting it must have been for her to be falling in love with three people instead of just one.

This all makes sense on a logical level. But it's not something my emotions allowed me to really absorb for a really long time. And even now my heart still doesn't quite know what to do with the concept of a stranger mothering my children. But she's a nice woman who cares about my kids. She loves my ex in a way I never could, which my ex deserves. She's the best-case scenario for our scenario.

If you are in a similar scenario, where a new person has come into your kids' lives, try to remember what it must be like for them to be entering into a family that is already in motion. They may fumble through trying to find their place, they may overstep or annoy, but it's not an easy thing to put your heart on the line by caring for someone else's children. Grace is not the easiest emotion to access when we feel like someone is encroaching on our kids, but if you can allow even a glimmer of it, it will serve all of you very, very well during what can be a very, very turbulent time.

• • • •

Not long ago the kids had an open house at their school. The kids, my ex, the girlfriend, my parents, and I all walked into the kids' classrooms together. Afterward, my son gave my ex a hug goodbye and pulled me into the hug too, because group hugs are his favorite. Then my daughter joined. Then my ex pulled the girlfriend in as well.

And there we all were, this messy modern family, hugging in front of the school. Probably confusing the hell out of anyone trying to do the math on what was happening. I'm not sure I've figured out the math myself, if I'm being honest.

Years have passed since this new woman entered my children's lives. We are at soccer games and birthday celebrations and school events together frequently. She's an important part of the kids' lives and will continue to be as they get older. And yet. She is still a complete stranger to me, and I am a complete stranger to her as well.

I hear about families where the parents and stepparents and bonus parents and kids all get along smashingly well, and I so envy their lack of pretense. Because I'm exceedingly bad at pretense. After so many years faking my way through my marriage, it grates on my soul to put on yet another mask when we are all together. I had genuinely hoped that this next chapter would provide the kids with something closer to authenticity.

I'd love to say we are one of those families that made it to the other side through the sheer force of our maturity and commitment to our kids. I keep waiting for the time when grace outweighs the preconceived notions that we've all ingrained into our opinions of each other. When humanity overcomes history and we open up to the possibility of something beyond pretense. But I have a feeling I'll be waiting for a while.

What I can say for sure is that we all show up. Over and over again, with smiles on our faces, we show up for our kids, because there is absolutely no pretense in how we all feel about our little humans. And maybe that's the best we can do for this particular chapter. Maybe landing somewhere between high fives and blatant animosity is not a horrible place to reside after the implosion of a family unit.

Of course, you may be the first one to partner up, and if you do, take this chapter to heart as an example of some of the emotions it may cause in your ex. Also, I highly recommend keeping your kids out of the equation for as long as possible, because once you involve them in your dating life, you are opening a can of worms that might be better left sealed until your new relationship has some time to establish itself independent of your old entanglements.

If you are trying to navigate a new person in your kids' lives, whether it be your ex's new person or yours, I hope my tales of extraordinary mediocrity and general emotional immaturity inspire you. It can be hard to compare yourself to the extremes of the shiny perfect blended families or the restraining order situations, so I offer you my story to demonstrate that maybe there is someplace in between for you, just like there was for us.

Show up, keep showing up, and try to give your heart time to catch up to your brain when it comes to the new math of your family post-divorce. I can't promise you the equation will ever make sense, but I know for sure that your kids are worth figuring out a way to make it all work.

Flip Your Perspective

While you might prefer your ex lead a miserable life of solitude for the rest of their days, your ex may well end up with a new person. And there is a chance this new person is going to become a part of your life as well. So, you need a strategy beyond blind rage when dealing with them. I suggest a flip in perspective. If and when you meet face to face, you have some options for what you can say, which is a perfect opportunity to practice your flipping. Let's practice some different scenarios now.

What you want to say:

"Let me tell you all the things that are horrible about my ex. Trust me, you want to know what you are getting into."

What you should say instead:

"Godspeed."

———

What you want to say:

"Don't try to buy my kids' love with presents, they are my kids, they cannot be purchased with things."

What you should say instead:

"Here is the kids' Amazon wish list. Go crazy. This is going to save me so much money."

———

What you want to say:

"You really believe the story my ex is telling you about our marriage?"

What you should say instead:

"Bless your heart." (Shout out to Jennifer Garner for this one.)

———

What you want to say:

"Stay in your lane."

What you should say instead:

"What podcasts have you listened to about parenting? All my education has been hands on, I'd love to hear what the experts have to say."

———

What you want to say:

"Listen, you *@#%#$@#$ . . . "

What you should say instead:

"Wild weather we're having, ammi right?"

DIVORCE SQUAD

New Math

"I was so relieved when my ex finally found a girlfriend. It got his attention off of me, which was such a relief. When we were all together I would introduce his new wife as my daughter's 'other mom' because I wanted her to know that what she was doing was important and she should take it seriously."

....

"The new wife has no kids, but has quite a few opinions on how my children should be raised. Thanks for your judgment, but I've been doing this for a minute, I think I know what I'm doing."

....

"There was a lot of my ex constantly throwing it in my face that they were partnered up again and I wasn't. Because getting into a new relationship five minutes after a divorce is definitely the healthier route to take."

....

"My ex, my new husband, and I are all on a group text together. The guys get along great."

....

"Maybe other people get over it, I mean I've gotten way better, but it still hurts to feel like you are competing against another person for your kids. My daughter is a grown-up real person now. She lives in Idaho, she just came to visit. She usually stays at her dad's house. And I know that she stays there because her dad has a whole bedroom that she can stay in and she doesn't have to sleep on a sofa. Logic! But every single time, it hurts. She's a grown-ass adult! What the hell is wrong with me?"

....

"My ex's new wife would insist on parenting my kids in ways that completely abandoned how we had always parented our kids. It was annoying and insulting. She had kids of her own, and when her ex-husband got re-married things got a little bit better. She finally realized what it felt like to have another woman intruding on parenting her kids, so she eased up with my kids."

....

"Look, the new girlfriend seems good for him, which is good for our daughter. I have no idea what the woman sees in him, but God bless her."

FUCK YOU, YOU FUCKING FUCK (A TIME FOR JOURNALING)

This Is Not Okay

Divorce is super common, and it can be comforting to know you aren't the only one whose marriage has imploded. But at the same time divorce is so common it barely registers as a blip anymore.

"Jane and Bill are getting divorced."

"Oh, really? That's too bad. But it makes sense. Did you see that overtime game last night? That was wild!"

Meanwhile Jane and Bill are over here dealing with what feels like a lot more than just a little blip, but they don't believe there is room to acknowledge the enormity of what they are experiencing. They pull themselves up by their bootstraps, put their heads down, and handle their business, because that's what is expected of them. People do this all the time, it's not a big deal, right?

Our culture is big on getting people to "okay" as soon as possible. A kid falls down, and the first thing we say when comforting them is, "It's okay, buddy, you're going to be okay." A similar thing happens when your life implodes. Your friends show up on your doorstep with booze and a firm promise, "It's all going to be okay, just give it time!"

Divorce and co-parenting and single finances and rebuilding a life are all extremely common. People do them every day, and you will do them too. But that doesn't mean they are easy, and it doesn't mean that you shouldn't be allowed to acknowledge how fucking hard they are.

You are strong and capable and absolutely will be okay, but sometimes it's healthy to look around at the clusterfuck of your life and yell, "This is NOT OKAY, I am NOT OKAY, and I don't need anyone blowing sunshine up my ass telling me that it's all going to be okay, because today it is most certainly NOT OKAY! Thank you for your prompt attention to this matter."

On the off chance you don't feel comfortable screaming that sentiment at the top of your lungs in the middle of your local Target, head on over to your journal and yell onto the page about all the bullshit that is most definitely not okay about life post-divorce. (Between the security guards and the dollar bins at Target, journaling may prove to be a safer option for this exercise.)

ALL THE THINGS THAT ARE NOT OKAY ... _____

_____

_____

_____

_____

_____

_____

_____

_____

_____

_____

13

You'll Miss the Towels Most of All

*(losing 50 percent of everything, just because
you lost 100 percent of one person)*

When I first left my marriage, I felt like a college student who had just moved into my first apartment. I set up a card table and folding chairs in my dining room and assembled Ikea furniture in the kids' rooms. I had a cheap set of pots and pans and exactly four plates. My mom gave me a presto wood bookshelf and bought me some new silverware. I was forty-two years old.

When a buddy came over to help me with a house repair, he asked me to go grab a screwdriver.

"I don't have a screwdriver."

"You don't have a screwdriver? What kind of lesbian are you?"

"A divorced one."

Another friend was over at my house, and we were trying to decide what to cook for a dinner party.

"How about burgers?"

"I don't have a barbeque anymore."

"Lasagna?"

"Let me check. Nope, I don't have a baking dish."

"We could just order takeout for everyone."

"We are going to need to get some paper plates, I don't have enough real plates for everyone."

And so it went. I had somehow gone from a fully functional adult to someone who couldn't say for sure if I owned a can opener (I didn't).

There is probably something empowering to be said about literally rebuilding your life, one screwdriver at a time. About the process of realizing that you have never felt more whole, even though you've technically lost so much. About discovering the value of peace over the value of things.

Lots of inspirational posters could be written about all of this, I'm sure.

But. If we are being honest, it's all a pretty big pain in the ass. I remember walking into my closet before a shower and realizing I had lost custody of my favorite towel in the split. Yes, I could easily buy a new towel, that was not the issue. The issue was that I really liked that towel, I'd already purchased that towel, and that towel was worn in perfectly; a new towel wouldn't be the same. I'd checked "towels" off my adulting list years prior. The same as I'd done with screwdrivers, plates, barbeques, and dining chairs. And now, just because I wanted to lose 100 percent of one person, I was having to replace 50 percent of everything else in my damn house.

None of this was unexpected or unjust. But it was very, very tedious. I think that's where divorce really gets you, in the tedious details that have to be dealt with on top of all the monumental details. You have to figure out custody schedules, and mediators, and budgets, and moving, and emotions, and healing, and *motherfucking screwdrivers*. The last thing you need after dropping your kids off at your ex's house, after an hour-long call with your lawyer, after paying all your bills with only half the income, after your therapy appointment, is to be standing in the kitchen and realize you can't actually make dinner because you don't actually own a can opener. Sonofabitch. The tiniest kitchen utensil can be what breaks your divorced back.

I have no real advice here, other than the promise that eventually your life will have all the pieces put back together again. With kitchen utensils and tools and towels and your heart all exactly where they are supposed to be. You'll reassemble piece by piece, the big pieces and the little ones. You can and will do this over time, and this time you'll be assembling a permanent structure.

Or, and this is actually becoming a real thing, you could create a gift registry for your divorce just like you registered for your wedding. Send out divorce announcements (see Chapter 2, "Divorce Announcements Should Be a Thing") to all your friends and family, and include a link to your registry at Target, "Good news is: I got out of a bad marriage. Bad news is: I lost my blender in the split. Please send help."

See if you can register for some therapy too, along with new towels, and you'll be all set.

14

The Wild West of Dating Apps

*(95 percent of profiles look like
the beginning of a true crime podcast)*

Tiger King is a reality show that came out during the peak of the 2020 COVID-19 quarantine. I think it's worth noting when it came out, because I believe the success of this batshit crazy show was tied directly to the overall absurdity that had befallen our country when we were locked down for months and told there was a deadly virus waiting in the air outside. We were not in our right collective state of mind, and somehow a show about a guy with a southern accent, several husbands, and a penchant for spooning with tigers became our national obsession. The apocalypse brings about a lot of unfortunate choices, it would seem.

If you are wondering how dating apps could possibly relate to *Tiger King*, then you probably haven't spent very much time on dating apps yet. Let me warn you about what you will discover if and when you go looking for love on the interwebs. First of all, go Google Joe Exotic, the star of *Tiger King*. The main images you will find include our boy rocking a bleached mullet, a sequined shirt, an eyebrow piercing, unfortunate facial hair, cowboy boots, and his arm around a full-grown tiger. I'm here to tell you that Joe Exotic would barely even register as odd if his images were to pop up on your Tinder feed. That's how amazing the world of online dating is.

Also, Joe's job as a tiger wrangler / deranged YouTuber and his penchant for marrying multiple men at one wedding? Sounds like the makings of a pretty solid online dating profile to me.

Now, contrary to what it may seem, I actually think dating apps are great. I know most people don't like them, and I can definitely understand why. It seems as though you have to swipe through hundreds of troubling profiles to find one that doesn't look like the beginning of a true crime podcast. And there's a 73.4 percent chance that the one "normal" profile is not actually a real person, but the beginning of a *Catfish* episode. The odds are grim, I'll admit. But! You really can't beat the efficiency of it all.

Technology is all about making our lives easier, and dating apps remove a lot of the work associated with humans' attempts to get laid (and/or find everlasting love, if you're into that sort of thing). Back in the olden days, we had to PUT ON REAL CLOTHES, go down to a bar, pay way too much money for shitty drinks, and yell over house music to whoever we might find attractive. And then, after all that, the lights would come on in the bar, or we would sober up, and we would immediately regret our evening activities. And if the lights didn't change our opinion, a few dates with this person would usually do the trick, "Wait, you still live with your parents??"

Now I just open my app, sober as can be, look through fully lit photos, and instantly weed out possible mates based on horrible grammar and/or concerning political rants. ALL WHILE WEARING SWEATPANTS. What a time to be alive.

It's also worth noting that, for the gays, apps are a really nice way to ensure we are (most likely—more on that later) connecting with people interested in our gender. I have no idea how to spot lesbians in the wild and definitely wouldn't have the nerve to approach a woman without knowing she is gay. So, apps are a nice safe(ish) place for me to swipe and interact.

I spent a lot of time on various dating apps following my divorce, and I'm here to share with you what I've learned while wading through the dating pool. While my pool may be a bit different from your pool, I tend to think horrible online dating profiles transcend all gender and sexual identities.

The People

I can swipe through a good twenty-five people on a dating app in less than a minute and get right back to watching my crap reality shows. Think of how long it would take me to decide not to date this many people in the real world. What a life I'm living over here.

The most troubling profiles in the women seeking women section of the dating apps . . . are men. What are these guys doing exactly? For men to show up on my app, they have to go into their settings and change their profile to "woman seeking woman." This is equal parts infuriating and inspiring. God bless men and their belief they can catch a lesbian on an off day and get her to entertain a change to her sexuality. The confidence!

Besides the overly confident men, dating apps also feature a lot of bi-curious women, couples looking for threesomes, and a lot of "free spirits" who are actually free from living in a house that isn't a van. There are filters and alarmingly long fingernails and more than the occasional confusing animal sidekick. There are also a lot of twentysomethings who could literally be my children, although I hope my children would wear clothing that is less revealing than these girls do.

Occasionally there are seemingly normal people, but more often than not I accidently swipe no on them, simply because I am in a swipe frenzy. (Which is probably for the best, since most true crime podcasts start with, "He seemed like such a normal guy. . . .")

After a while all the profiles start to run together, and I stop on only the most outlandish photos, just because they entertain me so.

Which leads us to . . .

The Photos

The Selfies

Selfies aren't innately bad, but the selfies on dating profiles seem to be intentionally bizarre sometimes. Why do people feel the need to take photos in the bathroom? Their home bathroom, public bathrooms, anytime there is a toilet nearby folks start thinking a photo session is in order. Whyyyyyyy? Is it the lighting? The mirrors? The chance that a complete stranger may walk in and see you admiring yourself in the loo? I just don't know.

The car has become another confusing photo location. So. Many. Car. Selfies. Do people get in their cars, catch a glimpse of themselves in the rearview mirror, and think, "Damn, I'm looking good today, let's get a photo of this." Only the speedometer knows for sure.

The Animals (Alive and Dead)

Of course people take photos with their dogs and/or cats. That's fine (except when *every single photo* includes the dog and/or cat, then I have some questions). Where things start getting interesting is the inclusion of more random animals.

Let me just tell you something that I need everyone to know. In my independent scientific studies, I've found that a statistically improbable number of lesbians own pet birds. It's a thing. Again, I'm not anti-bird, but I do wonder about someone who includes said bird in their main profile photo. I'm not sure I want to know what their living situation is like. Is the bird just flying free? Does it poop everywhere? Why IN THE HELL do you have a picture of you at a restaurant with a friggin' BIRD ON YOUR SHOULDER??

Birds aren't the end of the random. Guinea pigs, hamsters, lots of bearded dragons, a lemur, a llama, and the occasional turtle. One woman had a photo with her turtle on her chest. The turtle was wearing a homemade harness/leash. Exactly how fast is this turtle that it needs a leash??

Over on the male side of the apps (and occasionally with the females) there seem to be a lot more animals of the dead variety featured. Very large fish, deer, and the occasional pig. Who ever said men don't understand how to woo a woman? "Sleep with me, for I shall be able to provide food in the case of an apocalypse, m'lady!"

The Group Shot

I've found that there is one tried and true rule of dating apps (besides the lesbian/bird phenomenon) and it is this: if a person posts a group shot as their primary photo, the profile always, *always* belongs to the least attractive person in the group photo. Without fail. I'm not sure what the game plan is with this particular strategy, but I promise you I'm not going to post a photo on my dating profile of me with my more attractive friends. It's only a matter of milliseconds before someone clicks through my photos, hoping to date my hot friend, only to find that it's me that is looking for love. Cue disappointed sound effects, "Bah bah bahhh."

The Adventure

According to dating apps, every single human on the planet is in a constant state of adventure: climbing mountains, jumping out of planes, riding motorcycles, sunning on boats, zooming down ski slopes, traveling to far-off lands. Not a lot of photos of people in sweatpants ordering DoorDash for the seventh consecutive Friday night.

The Burning Man

Lots of people have gone to Burning Man and really, really want us all to know they have gone to Burning Man.

The Flex

Flexing can be literal, as in there are a lot of images of people working out or otherwise highlighting their very chiseled physique. There are also the materialistic flexes. "Here I am just casually standing. Oh, this luxury car? This old thing? Weird that it's in the photo too!"

The Super Deep and the Super Shallow

The personal descriptions on dating apps really run the gamut from nothing to manifesto. But my favorites are the super deep: "You're at home in your body and together our bodies spiral stardust." Or the super shallow: "Love to lol and have fun."

The Filters

Some of these photos are so filtered I can barely make out a nose on these women's faces. Do they realize that the point of dating apps is to eventually actually go on a real-life date? Like in person? Your future date will eventually find out you have a nose, so please stop with the filters.

The Odd

It's very hard to stand out as odd on a dating app, but there are some people who seem to be trying really, really hard to win some sort of award for the most peculiar profiles. There are lots of very random cartoon filters on faces (like puppy noses or kitten ears) or photo frames filled with bizarre art. There was one woman with cartoon bats flying all around her, with the phrase, "I stand with bats" written across the bottom of her photo. Uh. Okay? There was a group photo, where everyone was wearing pink latex bodysuits. Full body, as in, everyone's head is covered too. This was the person's main profile photo. One woman was wearing a 1950s housewife getup—pearls and all—admiring her reflection in a large meat cleaver, with the description, "I came here to play my ukulele and suck toes, and my ukulele is out of tune." Another woman was doing a curtsey with a paper plate on her head, lit candles on the plate, with each of her arms poked through five large slices of ham.

Dating is going great, thanks for asking.

The Clues

These are my favorite photos. They seem normal upon first glance, but they hold a myriad of clues in the background. I've swiped no on very attractive people, simply because of the absolute disaster that I've seen going on in the background of their photos. Clothes piled high, garbage on the floor, uncleaned litter boxes, weapons lying around, posters taped to the wall like a teenager. And all those bathroom photos you are posting? I'm looking at how organized your bathroom is as much as I'm looking at you.

Only Photos

These people think they are attractive enough to get dates without actually writing anything at all in their profile; their beautiful face is enough to inspire a yes swipe. Some of these people are correct, and some of these people really need to get to writing.

The Rules of Dating Apps

Dating apps can be a weird, scary place that often reflects a disturbing version of humanity. But they can also be a great way to meet people you may not otherwise get to connect with in the real world. To up your chance of success, follow these basic rules:

Actually Read

Don't just swipe yes on a cute face. Take the time to scroll down. Look for personality, punctuation, and anything that feels more authentic than, "I love to laugh." Yes, every human on the planet enjoys laughing, what else do you got?

Yes, and . . .

When you actually match with someone on a dating app, you need to use the initial messaging with them to really suss out whether this human is worth the effort of putting on real clothes and leaving the house. The biggest rule of app messaging is also the biggest rule of improv: "Yes, and."

In an improv performance, no one knows what the hell is going on, but for the show to work, everyone has to be willing to go along with whatever the hell is going on. A fellow performer will throw you a prompt like, "Hey, the beach sure is nice today." You might have wanted to do a bit about a doctor's office, but that's not what is happening. You can stop the momentum of the show if you respond with, "You know, I'm at the doctor's office, I'm not sure why you are mentioning the beach." The whole show has gone to shit because you can't just go with the flow. The first rule of improv would compel you to instead respond with, "Yes, the beach is nice. And! That couple over there seems to think it's a nude beach, what should we do?"

With that response you have (1) validated your scene partner's suggestion and then (2) kept the scene going by introducing more things that you can talk about.

It is somewhat baffling to me how few people understand this very basic structure to carrying on an engaging conversation.

I always lead with an anecdote about something, then throw out a question for the other party. If the other party only answers my question, without then asking me a question in return . . . they are shit at conversations, and no one will ever enjoy dating them. I have a two-message rule with this.

Meetup

When I first started on the apps, I would text back and forth forever with people before meeting up. I had this fairy tale playing out in my mind, where we were falling in love via the written word, like lesbians of lore. I thought I found my wife roughly eight times via text messaging, only to meet up in person and realize that speaking real words in real life to each other didn't have quite the same spark. Now I'll message someone back and forth for a day or so before asking to meet up, which can seem quick, but nothing beats an in-person vibe check. So do yourself a favor and don't wait long for the face-to-face portion of this little dance.

Be Honest

Don't waste other people's time. If you are just out of a relationship and not really looking for anything serious, be up front about that. If you meet up with someone who says they are looking for something casual and you are ready to get married next week, let the person know you have a U-Haul waiting in the parking lot.

If your idea of getting out into the wild consists of going to an actual store instead of shopping online and your match is someone who loves to camp, don't pretend you are an outdoor adventurer. That shit is going to catch up with you on the side of a friggin' mountain somewhere.

One of my Divorce Squad was horrified that a guy on her dating app put in his description that he is into pegging. I, on the other hand, thought it was awesome that he put that info in his profile. Get that out in the open right off the bat. He didn't wait until Date #3 or after sleeping with a girl. He put it right out there and didn't have to worry about revealing it later. I respect the honesty.

No Ghosting

If you go out with someone more than a couple of times and just aren't feeling it, don't ghost the poor soul. Drop them a text saying you aren't feeling it and you wish them the best. It's the right thing to do. I don't think this is necessary after a first date, unless they reach out to you requesting a second date. If they do, let them know that you didn't feel a connection. This will bum them out, but they will get their no and move on with their lives, instead of wondering if maybe you might randomly message back with a yes someday.

15

Belly Flopping
Into the Dating Pool

*(dating has changed since the last time
you were on the market)*

Putting yourself back out into the dating world is one of the most daunting tasks you'll tackle post-divorce. It's been a minute since you've had to engage in the tedious ritual of auditioning potential mates, and in that minute things have changed quite a bit. There are new acronyms and sexual identities and STDs to contend with now. So much fun!

I know for a lot of people dating is the final frontier of their divorce journey. They keep putting it off because they can't imagine starting something new or even flirting with the idea of casual dating. Maybe they were blindsided by their divorce and don't feel steady enough to venture out into the world. Maybe their failed relationship has made them a bit gun-shy about all humans in general. Maybe the thought of starting over at Date #1 is just too daunting of an undertaking to consider after the long journey they just took.

I get it, I do. But dating can also bring a little levity to your life. Putting yourself out there and going on some dates with different people is a fun way to reconnect with a version of yourself that existed before life got so serious. You don't need to be looking for your next spouse; you can just be looking for some good conversation, a few nice meals, and maybe a little making out. Sounds like a decent Tuesday night to me.

The dating world had an added layer of unease for me because I never actually dated women before spending twelve years with one. I dated men throughout my twenties, then settled down with the first woman I dated (highly do not recommend this strategy). Post-divorce I was looking forward to having the opportunity to date more women, but I was also very intimidated to be diving into a completely different dating pool.

Dating men was pretty simple. Meet a dude, go on dates, evaluate sanity and hygiene, and so on. There weren't a lot of things to consider with men besides compatibility and general chemistry. But with women things got decidedly more complex. Because women are decidedly more complex creatures.

Have you heard of the Kinsey scale? Admittedly dated, it is meant to illustrate the fluidity of sexuality. The scale ranges from zero to six, with zero meaning a person is exclusively "heterosexual" and six representing exclusively "homosexual." Professor Alfred Kinsey believed we all exist somewhere on this scale and that it's rare for humans to be 100 percent gay or straight.

I'm here to tell you that women tend to bounce all over that damn scale. Which makes it quite interesting to be a woman dating women. Let's just say, when dating men I never had to ask, "So, how long have you been dating women?" (Although, to be fair, some men did inspire the curiosity simply because of their ineptitude.)

On my dating adventures I came across straight women, bi-curious women, bisexual women, pansexual women, nonbinary people, and good old-fashioned lesbians. Lesbians seemed almost quaint compared to the other options available. I learned early on to avoid the straight and bi-curious women who contacted me, because those connections rarely ended well. I'm sure some of those women were on a road to real self-discovery, and I wished them the best, but after a couple of bad experiences, I was no longer interested in being a lesbian tour guide to those who were just passing through Gay Town.

I was also bombarded on the dating apps by polyamorous and ethically nonmonogamous women. Ethically nonmonogamous means that both partners are okay with the other not being monogamous. These women were already *very* happy in their primary relationships but were looking for flings or possibly additional relationships to complement their *very* happy partnerships. I have a lot of admiration for the polyamorous/ENM folks, because I simply cannot fathom trying to juggle relationships with more than one person at a time. That seems like more calendar and emotional coordination than I have the capacity to take on. Count me out.

There was also an endless supply of couples looking for a "unicorn" to come over and have a threesome with them. I wasn't sure what a horned mythical creature had to do with sexual escapades, but I was not curious enough to find out.

Once I sorted through all the different sexualities and dating preferences, I was able to find several women I was actually interested in getting to know better. This exercise had mixed results. In the beginning I made a point to only date women who offered the polar opposite of what I'd experienced in my marriage. These dates were like a breath of fresh air. There were hours-long intellectual discussions, hikes and bike rides, and just the general excitement of discovering new minds and bodies.

I got lucky and had a great chemistry with the first couple of women I dated. But since I had been out of the dating game for so long and had never even been in the dating game with women, I had no idea how rare these connections were. I took them for granted and blew them up pretty quickly.

Then I tried to lean into casual dating and open myself up to more second and third dates even if there wasn't a real connection happening. I was single and free and thought I should have a little fun. Go team! This effort was very short lived.

I had quite a few options for how to spend the 50 percent of time that I wasn't with my kids. There were friends and hobbies and writing and well, Netflix. I was in my forties, and if I'm being honest, dinner with a good friend or even a night alone binge-watching a solid Netflix show was a lot more appealing than going on a second date with a woman I knew wasn't a potential long-term connection. I was old enough to trust my gut, and I didn't have much interest in wasting my or anyone else's time on dates that were leading nowhere.

I tried my hardest to connect with the women I went out with, but I was also not willing to force anything or overlook glaring red flags simply because having a girlfriend would be fun. One woman was very engaging via text, but once we were face to face, she said almost nothing. At one point during dinner, I took a long chewing pause just to see if she would jump in to fill the silence. She did not. On the flip side, a different woman barely took a breath the entire time we were at coffee. Every time she took a sip of her caffeinated beverage I worried that her brain may short-circuit from the added stimulant.

Another date was allergic to pretty much every food on the planet. This was not her fault, obviously, but I couldn't figure out how I could possibly do life with a person who was both vegan and gluten intolerant. My life is very appetizer focused; I need a partner who shares the same passions. One woman had just left her husband two months prior after realizing she was gay. She sobbed on our first date. Another woman did my entire astrological chart over drinks to figure out if we were a match. The stars said no, as it turned out.

Then there was me, the only constant in all these failed connections. I was nervous on the first few dates, stumbled over my words, bitched about my ex too much, or tried to oversell myself. I was self-conscious about my marriage baggage and my mom bod. I came on too strong with the women I liked and was too quick to discount those who didn't give me instant butterflies. I told myself I wanted to find a partner, but I was nowhere near comfortable with actual vulnerability. I got really good at telling the same set of stories and background stats over and over again, each time becoming a little more disconnected from the process. I felt a bit like a Broadway performer who had to go out and put on the same show night after night. I rarely got a standing ovation, though.

Another added bonus to my dating adventures was that they were occurring during a global pandemic. I was trying to figure out how to meet up with strangers while the rest of the world was locked in their houses, sanitizing their groceries for fear of catching the plague. So that was fun.

The pandemic led to a lot of FaceTime first dates as well as socially distanced outdoor dates. Some dates didn't happen at all because the women had jobs that put them in way too much contact with other humans. One particularly nice woman told me she was a respiratory therapist. To which I replied, "So . . . you just spend twelve hours a day with COVID patients?" And that was the end of that correspondence.

When dates went well and progressed, the two of us would have to do the pandemic dance of whether it was safe to hug or kiss or sleep together. There was a risk assessment that went into even the smallest contact, which made any contact super, super sexy, let me tell you. At one point a woman I was dating tested positive for COVID, which meant I had to alert everyone in my life that I had possibly exposed them to the plague. Dating always involves the possibility of catching an STD, but COVID provided the unique opportunity for these kinds of conversations: "So, mom, the person I'm sleeping with has COVID, which means my sex life could potentially kill you. Sorry about that." Such an exciting time to be single and mingling.

Since I had been out of the dating game for so long and faced an abundance of obstacles (of both the pandemic and general human interaction variety), I needed a lot of help getting myself date-ready. Luckily for me, I was offered an abundance of aid from friends who knew I could not be trusted to navigate romantic entanglements without assistance. From my boobs to my clothes to my communication skills, these friends got me ready to date again. Here are a few of the people who came to my aid.

My Dating Advisory Committee

Coach

Damon is one of my best friends and also a bit of a ho. I have known him for over ten years, and in that time I don't think

I've ever heard a normal dating story come out of this man's mouth.

He is always dating three to four women at a time, and his dating life often sounds like the plot of an HBO comedy that probably wouldn't make it on air because it's way too over the top. Samantha Jones has got nothing on my boy.

Damon has *a lot* of experience dating women, so he became my dating coach as I ventured into the female side of the dating pool. His role involved a lot of cheering me on from the side-lines ("I promise you, your boobs look great, no one cares that you breastfed two babies."), swapping dating stories ("Tell me everything about the girl with great abs."), and giving me advice on how to attract women ("Have you tried just hanging out at the grocery store? Ladies just come up to me and ask me out at the grocery store all the time. I'm blessed.").

Fashion Consultant

Look, I know not all gay women are fashion challenged, but this one is. Without help I would end up wearing the same three outfits and two pairs of shoes for the rest of my life, and it turns out functioning adults don't do that. Make a note of it.

I worked from home and had been momming for a decade, so I basically had a closet full of sweatpants, hoodies, old T-shirts, and three bridesmaid's dresses. Pretty sexy stuff. Perfect for a pandemic. Not so much for venturing out into the dating world. Since I am also shopping challenged, I signed up for a monthly fashion delivery box. The box arrived every four weeks with roughly five pieces of clothing that were picked by people who were put on this planet to spread figure-flattering floral patterns to the masses. I would keep the pieces I liked and send back the rest, each month building my wardrobe into that of a person who actually socializes in person with other adult humans.

The stylists got to know my preferences and would try to tailor their selections to my tastes. In the beginning, I could tell that my stylist was attempting to push me, with more adventurous options. I sent her a note saying, "I'm a gay soccer mom, adventurous is not happening in my wardrobe."

I also enlisted my friend Jill as my fashion consultant. The two of us would play a little game called *Straight Eye for the Gay Girl*. She helped me shop for clothes and also provided consultation via text every time I tried to assemble said clothes in an acceptable way.

I'd send her a picture of me wearing a new pair of shoes with capri pants. She'd text back, "Lose the socks." I sent her a picture of a new floral shirt that came in my fashion box, "Does this look like I'm wearing curtains? I feel like I'm wearing curtains." She texted back, "Yes. But curtains are in style, so it works." Sometimes I'd send her just an image and she would text back just a word: "No."

And so on and so forth. Without Jill and my fashion boxes, I would have been out there trying to impress women while wearing jeans, a hoodie, and flip-flops. I'm forever grateful to the straights for their help in this area.

Mentor

I was not the first of my friends to navigate dating again after being partnered up for years and years. Thankfully, my good friend Lisa had already traveled the bumpy dating-after-divorce road and had plenty of advice to offer me on my new journey.

Her two biggest pieces of advice were (1) don't bother dating, it sucks, and (2) if you are going to date, make sure you are demanding great sex.

Lisa and I were texting one night about our various dating escapades, and she mentioned that her life had been dramatically changed when she connected with a woman who sold sex toys. When I asked her what she bought from the sex lady, Lisa texted, "Rubber ducks and lube and stuff." As we continued to text back and forth I was trying my *hardest* to figure out how rubber ducks were used as sex toys. I didn't want to seem like a prude, but the mechanics were just not computing in my head.

Finally, I gave up, "What are you supposed to do with the ducks??"

"Oops! I meant dicks. Rubber dicks."

That made a lot more sense.

Lisa was similar to Coach Damon in that she had a lot of experience on the dating scene, and I often reached out to her for advice. Her advice, however, had a decidedly softer tone to it than what I heard from Damon. When I needed to break it off with a woman I'd only been hanging out with for a couple of weeks, Damon advised, "Just stop returning her texts, she'll get the hint, then you don't have to hurt her feelings." This felt shitty to me, and Lisa agreed: "Be honest, tell her you aren't feeling it and wish her well. We are all adults, she'll understand, and it's better than leaving her hanging."

I agreed with Lisa, but I was debilitatingly bad at breaking up with people. I drafted several breakup texts in the Notes app on my phone and sent them all to Lisa for review. She finally replied with, "Oh my GAWD, just break up with the girl already! You are overthinking it!!"

Between her ducks and her advice, Lisa never steered me wrong.

Teammate

Anna was a fellow mom on roughly the same divorce timeline as me. We corresponded often about our life implosions and our (mostly failed) attempts at dating. I'd complain about the number of bi-curious women on the dating apps, and she'd counter with the number of men who had sent her unsolicited dick pics. We'd check in on the progression of each other's relationships and give advice as needed.

It was nice having another person to chat with who was also juggling middle-aged divorce, dating, and parenting. We'd commiserate about our kids and jobs as well as our bad dates and annoying exes. Our coffee dates were much more entertaining than most of my painful first dates, if I'm being honest.

••••

I highly recommend you assemble your own Dating Advisory Committee as you venture back into the world post-divorce. The whole endeavor can be really intimidating, and you are going to need all the help you can get. You are a completely different person than when you were single and mingling previously. You may have even forgotten how to human with anyone you didn't give birth to.

But I promise you, it's just like riding a bike. If riding a bike involved trying out twenty bikes with flat tires before maybe finding one that could possibly make it a couple miles before the pedals fell off. But the point is! You can do this! And as the first official member of your advisory committee, I will now share with you my handy dating tips (sorry, you are on your own in the fashion department).

Advice for Dating After Divorce

Relax

Take a deep breath and let go of all of your expectations. Not every person you meet is going to be THE ONE, and that is OKAY. Use your first few dates to find your footing and try not to build them up in your head as anything more than practice rounds. Get reacquainted with small talk and polish the Cliff's Notes version of *My Life Until Today*.

Keep It Casual

Don't overcomplicate first dates. Think coffee or tea or some other casual public place. Give the two of you the opportunity to connect and get to know each other without the pressure of a well-orchestrated date or even an entire meal. If it's going well, you can sit and chat for hours; if it's a bust, you aren't obliged to make it through dessert before calling the time of death.

Have Fun

This goes hand in hand with the advice to relax. Once you find someone who is worthy of Dates #2, #3, and beyond, don't forget to have fun. You've been in a committed relationship and taking care of kids for a long time, you deserve to let loose a little. Have lots of sex, go on random adventures together, definitely don't act your age. These dates may evolve into something more serious over time, but in the meantime, let your dating life be the one part of your world that exists just to make you smile.

Take Charge

Not everyone needs this advice, but I definitely did. Back in my twenties I was never the one to make the first move on dates; I was way too intimidated for such things. But when I started dating women, the dynamics changed a bit, and I was forced to take charge on some dates because neither one of us wanted to appear too forward. I highly recommend you take charge as well, no matter who you are dating. Life is short, kiss the people you want to kiss. If you are feeling a connection with someone, there's not much sexier than looking them in the eye and asking, "Is it okay if I kiss you?"

Don't Chase

If I teach you only one thing as you head out into the dating world, let it be this: anyone who wants to spend time with you will make time for you. Let's repeat it for those in the back. **Anyone who wants to spend time with you will make time for you.** Full stop.

You may meet a person out in the dating world who feels like they most definitely could be THE ONE. You get butterflies in your stomach when you think about them, you have so much fun when you are together, you can't wait to see them again. But. They aren't the quickest to get back to you. They tell you they have a really busy schedule, and they seem to have a hard time fitting you into that schedule. You are the one who always instigates the contact and plans.

Let me be straight with you: That person is not THE ONE. THE ONE has butterflies for you too and is also excited to see you again. Everyone has busy lives, but people

make time for the things that are important. If you are important, your person will make time for you. You should not have
to chase them down.

Respect is important in a relationship, and it should be a
part of the relationship from Day 1. If a person is flaky or bad at
communication or standoffish . . . they are not respecting you
or your time. And you are too damn old to be chasing disrespect-
ful people. Bid them good day and be on your way.

Don't Settle

One of the biggest reasons I started taking charge on dates was
because a kiss could tell me a whole lot about whether there
would be more dates with this particular human. I had several
dates that went smashingly well, only to end with a really, really
bad kiss. Could I have pushed forward and tried to make it work?
Yes. Am I too damn old to be trying to force things into working
on Date #2? So many yeses. As I mentioned, life is short. Don't
waste it settling or trying to force things to fit. When it's right,
you'll feel it. You've been through too damn much to settle for
anything less than a resounding yes from your gut.

Don't Love Bomb

But! Even after your gut gives its approval, you can still take
your time. There's no need to rush anything in a new relationship, and you should be cautious with anyone who tries to speed
things up too quickly.

Early on in my dating lessons, I learned about a common
dating hazard called "love bombing." Love bombing happens at
the beginning of a relationship, when everything is still in the

very heightened, exciting period. Apparently, some people really enjoy going all in during this period; promises are made, futures are planned, love is dropped like bombs all over the place. And then after a few months, the excitement wears off for one or both partners, and it becomes obvious that this love assault is not sustainable.

Be careful not to drop love bombs, and try not to get wrapped up in someone else's bombing. Take things nice and slow, be realistic about who the two of you are together and how this thing could look long term. Breathe, have fun, and let things progress without the pressure of being SOMETHING BIG right away. You are probably still paying off your legal fees from your last SOMETHING BIG, so maybe take a minute to let this one evolve slowly. . . .

DIVORCE SQUAD

Dating Lowlights

"He didn't even try to kiss me for the first five dates. My friends told me to just go in for the kiss on Date #6 because he was obviously really shy or really gay. Turns out . . . I think he was both."

....

"I've been proposed to three times. I knew every guy less than a month."

....

"There have been a lot of guys who were married but didn't say anything until we met up."

....

"On our third date she made me dinner at her house. During dinner she said, 'You belong in this house.' Trust me, dinner wasn't that good."

FUCK YOU, YOU FUCKING FUCK (A TIME FOR JOURNALING)
Red Light, Green Light

As you head out into the dating pool, it is important that you establish who exactly you are looking to swim with. You just got out of a bad relationship, and you don't need to jump into anything new unless it's a good fit from the start.

But how can you know for sure who is a good fit? Well, you can start by thinking hard about this subject well before you begin going on actual dates. Dates can be fun and light and boozy and kissy. And once fun and booze and kisses come into play, logic can make its departure from the proceedings. On a date, you may be sitting across from a sweet smile or a particularly chiseled physique. Pair that with a wine buzz, and you may completely overlook the fact that this person hasn't stopped talking about cryptocurrency for forty-five minutes straight.

So. We have to get out ahead of the wine buzz.

In this journaling exercise we are going to list out all the personality traits we are looking for in a new match as well as the personality traits that will most likely lead us into another dumpster fire. We are too old to be putting out fires, and we are too smart to believe there is any hope of changing anyone else's personality.

Be honest and brazen and bold in making these lists. Obviously no one human is going to have every positive quality you are looking for, but the mere act of writing them down will help you figure out what it is you are actually seeking and what it is that you've been missing for so long.

Also, list every single thing that drove you insane about your ex, and be honest about which of those traits would most likely be toxic to you again. Highlight those traits, underline them, revisit them often in your dating life. Humans are creatures of habit, and there is a good chance you may end up attracted to someone who is a lot like your ex, simply because they are familiar. Check in with this list and with your gut often, to avoid another disaster.

GREEN FLAGS

List all the personality traits you fantasized about while you were stuck in a marriage with your ex. Explore with abandon.

_____

_____

_____

_____

_____

_____

_____

_____

RED FLAGS

List your ex's personality traits that annoyed the shit out of you.
Avoid at all costs.

_____

_____

_____

_____

_____

_____

_____

_____

List any other traits that are also a hard no. If you happen across
someone who has one of these traits do not let their smile or
physique talk you out of your hard no.

_____

_____

_____

_____

_____

_____

_____

_____

16

The First Post-Split Relationship

(the poor soul who has to deal
with your broken ass)

In my chats with the Divorce Squad, I've found that the first serious post-divorce relationship tends to happen either *right after* the split (as in, the moving boxes are not even unpacked) or a *really long* time after the split (as in, these walls aren't coming down anytime soon).

Jumping into the next thing right away provides an excellent opportunity to completely ignore the wreckage from the last thing and, in an alarming number of cases, also provides a great way to get married again. Because apparently learning lessons is highly overrated.

In the case of the people who wait a really long time to get into a new relationship, they are usually way too gun-shy to even look in the direction of another thing because the last thing was such a fucking disaster. It's going to be a long time before they entertain the idea of another shit show, thank you very much.

In my case, I dabbled in both "Let's jump right into something new!" and "I'm gonna hold off a long minute before starting another party just yet."

Shortly after my ex announced her everlasting love for a woman she had known for roughly forty-eight hours, I went full force into searching for my own love story. I was swiping on dating apps with abandon, doing FaceTime "dates" on the regular, and driving multiple hours to meet up with potential rebound options. I wasn't quite sure what I was looking for, but I was sure I was open to whatever the dating gods had in store.

That general frame of mind led me to a date with a woman who told me from our first app interactions that she had never dated women before. Normally this would be a hard no for me, because straight girls never end well for lesbians. Trust me on that one.

But I was in a general "whatever" phase of my post-divorce dating life, and this woman seemed really cool. I'd go out with her a couple of times, maybe introduce her to the joys of being with women, and move right along. Easy peasy.

Cue narrator: "That is not what happened."

My first date with Julia involved talking for hours at a local restaurant. This was peak COVID times, so as we were leaving the restaurant I asked politely if I could give her a hug. She said yes, and that was when this casual "whatever" date became something more. When I hugged her, I got hit with a jolt, one that I've only felt a couple of other times in my life. This rare jolt hits me right in the ribs, but its meaning is usually found wandering around my heart. I held on to the hug for much longer than a person should hold on to a hug during (1) a first date and (2) a global pandemic. She held on too.

She walked me to my car, where we proceeded to talk for another hour in the dark parking lot. When it was time to go (because all the restaurants had closed and it was officially probably dangerous to be hanging out in a dark parking lot), I asked for another hug. That hug led to a kiss, which led to a teenage-caliber make-out session while standing in the parking lot. A dude in a big pick-up truck drove by and was pleasantly surprised by our immature choices.

As we spent more time together, I tried very hard to maintain my "whatever" stance, but it wasn't long before it was clear that my heart felt far from "whatever" about her. We had one of those fast-fire connections where the two of you say things like, "I can't believe we've only known each other two weeks." And other things like, "I know it's only been a month, but I think I'm falling in love with you."

You know, totally rational things.

••••

She scared me. The way I cared about her scared me. Being vulnerable scared me. So much so that I literally ran out of her house on more than one occasion when I felt a little too overwhelmed by the fear.

You know, totally rational things happening.

Neither Julia nor I was familiar with the number of emotions I was having about our relationship. I had been numb for years, and she had only been with men who weren't big on emoting. So, this was new territory for both of us. She was patient with me as I navigated my new feelings and my divorce drama.

I was still in the aftermath of my divorce explosion when Julia and I started dating. My ex and I were constantly fighting over every damn thing two people could think to fight about. I was living in a hotel. I was so. damn. tired. All the time. I wasn't sleeping or eating well, my stomach was constantly in knots. I'd lost a good twenty pounds off my already slim frame.

Julia made me happy; she was pretty much the only thing that made me happy during that time. Being with her blocked out all the other bullshit, and for a moment I could forget about the fact that I had lost 50 percent of my kids and 100 percent of my housing. So, I grabbed on to her like a buoy. I grabbed on way too tight.

I didn't realize it at the time, but I was depressed. I hid it well, and I didn't feel depressed when I was with Julia, but that was mostly because I would just fall into her and forget the rest of the world. It all sounds like a '90s love ballad, but in reality, that dynamic is not nearly as entertaining as Edwin McCain or Savage Garden would have had us all believe. Julia and I had a lot of fun together, but ultimately, being someone's buoy is exhausting, and she was no longer interested in the gig. After only three months of dating, Julia broke up with my broken ass. The ending of our very short-lived romance hurt me more than the end of my twelve-year marriage. Because I knew this end was mostly my fault.

When we broke up I was devastated, but I was also a little scared. I was already a mess from the previous few months (and years, if we're being honest). To put it frankly, I couldn't afford to have a proper breakdown over this breakup because I was already too far gone as it was.

So then.

I had a good cry.

And then I got to work.

I booked a therapy appointment (see Chapter 6, "All the Therapy"), I put on my running shoes, and I started taking melatonin at night. I began putting myself back together, because simply surviving was no longer enough (see Chapter 22, "New You"). It was time to be better.

Not long after Julia and I broke up, I was whining to one of my friends, "It was such a waste, I should have never dated her, the timing was awful."

To which my friend replied, "It wasn't a waste, and the timing was perfect. She came into your life exactly when you needed her."

I was listening to a lot of podcasters at that time, and one of my favorites was Esther Perel. She is a psychotherapist who studies and speaks about relationships and intimacy. I came across a quote of hers shortly after my breakup with Julia: "There are many people you will love, and they are not all necessarily the people you will make a life with. Are you looking for a love story or are you looking for a life story?"

I started to shift my perspective about my time with Julia. My friend was right. Julia came into my life exactly when I needed her. My numb heart hugged her in that dark parking lot, and she brought me back to life. She loved me during one of my most difficult times.

Yes, she broke my heart when she ended things, but even that turned out to be what I needed. I needed to change, I needed to be better, I needed to actually heal, not just Band-Aid my broken parts with a new person. And I couldn't and wouldn't have done any of those things until something shook me out of my sleepwalking state.

The biggest gift Julia gave me was showing me what I'm capable of feeling. After twelve years spent in an unhappy partnership, I thought maybe I just wasn't built for deep affection.

Julia reminded me that I am. And she also gave me a baseline for what to look for in future relationships.

And that baseline is what moved me into the waiting a *really long* time category of post-divorce relationships. After Julia I knew I was of little to no value to any possible partners, so I held off on dating for a while. Then I dated casually. Then I started only dating if the person seemed like they had long-term potential. That cut my dates down tremendously and also resulted in a lot of early breakups.

Julia jolted me and reminded me that I'm capable of real connection, so now I am not willing to accept anything that is less than exhilarating. Which means I'm going to have to wait. I'm okay with that now. I'm in no rush. I'll be ready when she shows up, and in the meantime, I'll be over here singing along to '90s love ballads at the top of my lungs.

Dos and Don'ts of That First Relationship

I don't recommend jumping right into a relationship post-split, because I've personally experienced how much can be discovered when we give ourselves the permission to embrace the idea that we can be whole without a partner. And what a better partner we can be for someone later if we are bringing a whole person to the table, instead of someone who is still in pieces.

But, at the same time, I know that life unfolds in mysterious ways. Sometimes when one door closes, a dating app opens, and who are you to argue with the universe and/or Tinder? So, if you are going to jump in, try your hardest not to belly flop onto the poor soul who has been tasked with the unfortunate job of catching you.

Do

Be Honest with People

Honesty is always the best policy when heading out into the dating world and definitely when moving from casual dates to something more serious. Tell people that you are fresh off a split, and let them decide for themselves if that's a disaster movie they want to be a part of. Be honest about why your marriage ended, own your part in it, and communicate what you plan to do differently in the future.

Be Honest with Yourself

Divorce is hard and sad and isolating. Dating is fun and happy and full of connection (emotional and physical). All that dating euphoria will be such a stark contrast to your previous failed relationship, and I'm here to tell you that euphoria is not known for producing the most rational of decisions.

So, be honest with yourself about this new person. They aren't perfect, I promise you that, because no one is. Keep your eyes open to who the two of you really are together, not just the version of yourselves that exists in the euphoria tornado of new love.

Be Selective

Post-divorce life can be very lonely (see Chapter 11, "All the Time in the World"). And loneliness can lead to an almost pathological desire to find a new person to spend time with.

But your time is way too valuable to be spending it with whoever happens along your path. Be aware that you may try to force something or someone to work just because you really don't want to be alone. Be selective about who you spend your time with, and don't be scared to cut people loose who aren't dazzling you.

Be Slutty

But, on the other hand, who doesn't enjoy a solid nonselective Ho Phase? (See also Chapter 5, "The Seven Stages of Divorce.") You've been through a lot, your divorce has left you feeling a little battered and broken, and what better way to recover than by randomly sleeping with several attractive strangers?

Not everyone you date needs to be a love story or a life story, or even a story that lasts more than twelve hours. Go out there and be slutty for a bit. Touch and be touched. Explore new bodies and delight in new people exploring yours. Tinder demands it.

Don't

Be Someone's Project

I'm gonna repeat this one in all caps: DON'T BE SOMEONE'S PROJECT. Just don't. Maybe your divorce has left you feeling broken. Maybe being with your new boo makes you feel like your pieces are being welded back together through the force of their love for you.

Stop it. Just stop. Because that's bullshit.

It's not your boo's job to weld you back together. You're the one who needs to do that work, because if someone else does

it, they are just going to end up MacGyver-ing your ass back together. There's no actual welding happening, only Scotch tape,
Elmer's glue, and a random paper clip.

Rush

You've done the marriage thing before, why on earth would you
want to rush into something again? Take things slow, be rational, let your new relationship breathe and become its own entity
beyond its distinction as The Rebound. If it's real, then you have
all the time in the world to make sure you've got it right. Take
that time.

Compete

Divorce can feel like a bit of a competition with your ex. You've
gone from doing life together to wishing failure upon each other.
Isn't love grand? Don't let your ex's love life or post-divorce relationship status influence whether you get into a relationship
of your own. Your ex rushing into something (see Chapter 12,
"Your Replacement") doesn't mean you need to as well, and your
ex being partnered up doesn't mean you need to grab the first
person you find and immediately turn them into your plus-one
to keep up.

Be Too Slutty

I'm all for having fun and letting go of inhibitions and embrac-
ing sexuality at any age. But I'm also a big fan of acknowledging why exactly superficial relationships feel so comfortable
post-divorce.

In my case, I started to realize that casual relationships felt a little too familiar to me. There was no emotional connection, and therefore I was risking nothing. That was fun for a little while, but as time went on, I realized I was not just having fun, I was actively avoiding engaging in anything that could potentially hurt my heart. And, for me, I was no longer interested in being that lazy.

Be Someone's Project

Hi, it's me again, reminding you that no one else on the planet is responsible for healing your broken parts. **Do your own work.** Thank you for coming to my TED Talk.

DIVORCE SQUAD

Sometimes It Works.
Sometimes Not so Much.

I chatted with two of my Divorce Squad about their post-divorce relationships. Bobby started dating a woman only a few months after his wife moved out. He went on to marry that woman. Teresa got into a serious relationship with a woman not long after her split, and the new relationship moved quickly. Even though Teresa really cared about her new girlfriend, it ultimately didn't work out.

Bobby:
"My friend set me up with his girlfriend's friend. I'd only been separated a few months, but honestly, my marriage had been dead for years. We hadn't slept together

in over a year. The emotional attachment to my wife was long gone.

"Meeting my new girlfriend didn't feel as quick as it seems, because I felt like I was done with my marriage for such a long time before we actually split up. It was so nice to be happy again, to connect with someone again. My ex-wife was not okay with me moving on so quickly, I think she thought I was her back-up plan if things didn't work out with the guy she left me for.

"I didn't expect to end up with someone so quickly, but I was open to it, and I'm glad I was."

Teresa:
"It was a situation where I knew she wasn't my person from the beginning. It really should've been a friendship, but she pursued me, and it felt comforting at the time. She's an incredible person, and I knew she would make a great partner and stepmom, but I just couldn't get there. It was hard to speak my truth, I'm not very good at being the 'dumper' in the relationship. It was a very important step for me to take after what happened with my ex-wife and the dynamics of our relationship (I didn't stand up for myself often, and she did a lot of gaslighting). I absolutely adore the ex I had right after my marriage, and she gave me an idea of what I truly wanted."

17

When the Law Gets Involved

(mediation, divorce lawyers,
forensic accountants! Oh my!)

In the thick of my divorce drama, when we were hammering out the details of our split, I consulted a very ruthless divorce attorney. I was not happy about the proposed distribution of our assets, and I was ready to go all in fighting for what I felt I deserved.

I shared our details with this attorney, who was a friend of a friend, and I expected him to be equally invested in my battle cry. Instead, he told me this: "Look, if you want to buy me a new boat, I'd be happy to take this case and fight it for you. But I think it would be a better choice for you to let all this bullshit go and move on with your life."

This was not what I was expecting to hear from a ruthless divorce attorney, but it turns out it was exactly what I needed to hear. I did not, in fact, want to buy this nice man a boat. It was, in fact, time for me to move on with my life.

Throughout our time together, Elizabeth and I had known a few couples who had paid their respective divorce attorneys hundreds of thousands of dollars during their split-ups. Elizabeth and I really, really didn't want to go that route. Lighting that much money on fire for no real reason was something we were both very committed to avoiding, and I think that commitment was what saved us from a long legal battle in the end. Whenever we started to go off the rails, we'd stop and really breathe in the reality of what it would mean to lawyer up for a fight, and neither of us was ever pushed far enough to take that step.

We had enough moving parts in our partnership (two kids, two businesses, five properties, not to mention multiple 401[k] accounts) that lawyers' eyeballs turned to dollar signs when they looked at our stats. Every aspect of our lives was so intricately intertwined that most legal professionals recommended hiring a forensic accountant as a first step in our dissolution. The job title "forensic accountant" sounds very fancy, and it turns out the cost of a forensic accountant sounds even fancier.

We agreed to mediation from the beginning, and we were able to stick with it until the end. That is not to say that our mediation went smoothly. In fact, we nearly broke our mediator the first time we met with him. This was a man who spends his entire professional life dealing with unhappy couples in the middle of divorce, and after one session with us, he said he wasn't sure if he was qualified to deal with our level of hostility. So, kudos to us for setting a new bar in this man's career.

Throughout mediation we'd push and pull and shout and pout. We'd spent years building this big life together, and there was no real way to break it into two without each of us feeling a bit ripped off in the process. But every time one or both of us would be tempted to abandon mediation, we were brought back to earth by words like "forensic accountant." Yes, we were both getting less than we should be getting, but to get a fair amount, we'd need to pay lawyers a stupid amount, and that would cut the fair amount back down to lower than what we would have gotten if we just settled for the less than fair amount.

So you see, it was just math.

And money wasn't the only part of the equation worth considering. The friends we knew who had spent hundreds of thousands of dollars on their divorces? It took them *years* to spend that much money. As in, they spent *years* fighting with each other, going back and forth through lawyers, pushing and pulling and shouting and pouting. I was definitely not a fan of lighting cash on fire via legal fees, but more than that, I knew my body and mind couldn't take a drawn-out battle with the person I had to see every three days at kid exchanges. Our marriage had already spent years flatlining toward its demise, and I was so, so tired. It was time to put us all out of our misery.

Because I was so tired, I moved us into hyperdrive. Within about a month we finalized our marital settlement agreement (MSA). It was not the funnest month, but we got it done.

I'm not sure I recommend my hyperdrive strategy, because in pushing so hard to wrap things up quickly, I added an element of pressure and chaos to a time that was already raw from our recent split. Of course, as I look back on it with the benefit of time and rational eyes, I can see that we really should have taken it slow and not been so reactionary in making such consequential decisions.

But that's the conundrum of a divorce settlement. It is very, very difficult to move on to anything resembling healing when the two of you are in the thick of hammering out an agreement.

There is way too much pushing and pulling and shouting and pouting going on for anyone to have anything near a rational perspective. Taking more time doesn't magically make the situation less raw; it merely extends the period of rawness. Something about divorce turns people into completely irrational versions of themselves, and no amount of time will alleviate that.

The TV show *Divorce Court* is not a realistic depiction of what divorcing actually looks like. If you want to get a more accurate representation, you will need to switch over to programming with interactions that are much more volatile than the mild disagreements on *Divorce Court*. Not boxing, because that is still a bit too civilized. What you really need is to turn on a WWE match to bring home the visual we are going for. WWE has large adults in full-body spandex pounding their chests, throwing chairs at each other, and flinging their bodies into clothesline midair tackles. This is what humans actually look like when they are in the middle of a divorce battle. Everything is heightened, emotions have taken all logic out of the mix, and tables are being hurled for no apparent reason.

One of my Divorce Squad described the moment she and her ex signed their divorce agreement, after nearly a year of lawyers and vitriol: "It literally started pouring down rain outside the second we signed the paperwork. We all felt it, this relief, and even the sky was done. It was finally over and we could finally move on."

I regret rushing our settlement agreement, especially because it was such a complete change of pace for my ex and she was left discombobulated by the new speed I demanded she keep up with. But I don't regret getting everything settled quickly and allowing us both to move into the next stage of healing from each other. The animosity that came from unraveling a life was absolutely toxic to my soul, and I knew in my ulcered gut that I needed it to be done as fast as possible.

As you make your way through the minefield of your MSA, I hope that you can make it to the other side of the battlefield sooner rather than later. Here are some of the ways I recommend surviving to tell the tale.

Find Rational Friends

As much as we all like to fancy ourselves mature adults, divorce has a way of turning cool heads into emotional powder kegs. The fact is, there is not enough incense in the world to counter this inner turbulence, but I highly recommend keeping one or two rational friends on speed dial throughout the process (see also Chapter 8, "Assembling Your Team").

Rational friends aren't always going to be your favorite, because, especially in the beginning, all you want to hear is, "I KNOW! You are RIGHT! They are an ASSHOLE. Let's fuck them all the way over! We ride at dawn!" And that kind of blind support definitely has its place.

But you also need the friend who isn't afraid to say, "I know you think they are an asshole, and I agree with you. Which is why they really aren't worth the amount of time and energy you are wasting on them. You have to let this shit go."

Rational friends love you, but they also love logic, and they aren't afraid to provide you a two-for-one deal. Hold on tight to these friends, because it's rare to find a person brave enough to be honest with you when you are refusing to be honest with yourself.

Consult with Attorneys

I always recommend going the mediation route if you can, but that doesn't mean you shouldn't check in with a lawyer and make sure there are no glaring issues you are overlooking. Most attorneys offer an initial thirty-minute consultation call for free, and I recommend you take a few of them up on that offer as you head out on your divorce settlement adventure.

I spoke to five attorneys during our split and even paid a few for an hour-long discussion so that I could understand the legalities of all our moving pieces. Divorce attorneys get a bad rap because they can be ruthless when fighting for their clients. But every single attorney I spoke to was actually really kind and helpful in talking me off several different ledges.

They know the landscape of the court system, and they know exactly how things will play out if you choose to walk away from the mediation table. They are in the business of winning, and they will be honest with you about whether there is any chance for anything resembling victory via lawyering up. They have no emotional connection to your life and as such are a great asset when it comes to being logical about a very emotional situation.

Do the Math

As I mentioned previously, there is math to be considered when deciding how hard you want to fight during your divorce. That equation involves both dollars and heartburn. To figure out your math, sit down with the help of a rational friend and/or a trusted financial advisor and really dive into the equation of your situation.

Make a list of all the things you want out of your divorce agreement. Be outlandish in your hopes. Then start circling the must-haves. Maybe put asterisks next to the ones you know your ex will fight.

What will that list look like if you make it a priority to get to an agreement early? How much will you lose out on financially or otherwise if you lean heavily into compromise? How many of your must-haves are nonnegotiable?

After your first mediation appointment, make a list of what was discussed as a possible agreement. Compare it to your dream list. Are the differences between the two big enough to head into battle? Ask an attorney for an estimate on time and cost for battle, write that down as well. Then take a look at everything and be honest with yourself about the best route forward for your mind, your bank account, and your stomach lining.

And when life gets tough, there's always a country song to light the way. Kenny Rogers never lets us down:

Know When to Hold Them

For some couples going the attorney route is simply the only option. There is absolutely no way the two of them will ever be able to work with a mediator and come to an agreement. I've known several couples who broke their mediators and were told after one session not to bother scheduling any more. Other couples couldn't even get on the same page long enough to agree on what mediator to use, which is not a great sign of future compromise. Some couples may really need the buffer of lawyers so that they can avoid any and all direct interaction with each other.

One of my Divorce Squad was a stay-at-home mom before her husband left her. She had put her career on hold for years to raise their kids and was going to have to completely rebuild her life from scratch following his abrupt decision. He owned a successful business and did everything in his power to keep her from getting any money in the split.

She had to borrow funds to hire an attorney to fight him. It was a long, drawn-out, messy process, but in the end, she got a fair settlement. Knowing that she pretty much broke even between the lawyer fees and the settlement, I asked her if it was actually worth it to have put all that money and effort into fighting.

"Yes!! Because he was trying to push me into a corner and pay me what he wanted to pay me, and the lawyer fought for what I deserved. More than that, though, it taught him that he can't just push me around. He seemed to respect me a little more afterward, which has made things better all-around in the years since."

Another Divorce Squad member really wanted to go the mediator route but ultimately realized it just wasn't going to work for his situation, "When we first talked about divorce, I convinced her that mediation was the best option for us. But she was just way too emotional for it. It's probably better that we have lawyers because she needs someone to temper her impulses and her lawyer seems to be doing that."

In the case of any sort of abuse, mediation is rarely a feasible option. One of my Divorce Squad figured this out very quickly in her efforts to mediate her divorce, "He was an emotionally abusive narcissist. After one session the mediator told me that there was just no way my ex was going to budge on anything. Mediation is impossible with a person like that, and it wasn't going to be a healthy situation for me either."

Only you know the dynamics of your relationship and what the short- and long-term ramifications will be when choosing between the mediator or lawyer route. Mediation is meant to be an easier process, but if it's not a viable option, there's no harm in accepting that early on and lawyering up for a fight.

Know When to Fold Them

One of my Divorce Squad spent years battling with his ex over how to split up the house they owned. He wanted to stay in the home, so he had to buy her out. He'd used inheritance money for the down payment, but she was not acknowledging that fact in determining how much he owed her. His bank statements didn't go back far enough to validate his assertion, and the issue became a he said / she said. He knew he was right and refused to give in.

Meanwhile, he was paying lawyer fees for *years* to go back and forth with his ex on this matter, and, here is the kicker, the property appreciated a good $100,000 during the time he refused to settle. This appreciation ended up costing him more than if he had just paid his ex what she was demanding in the beginning.

It's important to understand that the word "fair" can end up costing you a lot of money and heartburn during your divorce. I know this for a fact, because I have the empty Tums containers to prove it. I can totally relate to getting infuriated over perceived injustice, especially when you are being asked to accept an outright lie. That shit is unacceptable.

But at some point you might have to let go of the word "fair" and embrace the word "enough." As in, "I've had" and "This is gonna have to be."

Know When to Walk Away

When you look back at the list you made during your previous math lesson, there will come a point where you have to start removing line items. Hold on to your must-haves as long as you can, but also be realistic about how many are actually feasible. If the negotiations have reached a standstill, one or both of you is going to have to blink eventually. Check in with that rational friend and have them walk you through where you might be able to give a little.

Know When to Run

As soon as you arrive at a settlement, get that shit signed and get on with your life. Run, do not walk, to your next chapter. Put the signed agreement somewhere you can access it if needed, but unless your ex does something in blatant violation of your MSA, do NOT flip through it thinking about all the compromises you had to make, all the things you should have gotten, all the wrongs that were done in that document and in all the years that came before it. Just don't.

We are done festering. We are running away from that dumpster fire and are headed toward a trash-free life. Let's go.

18

Co-Parenting—Part 2

(you are in this for the long haul)

I firmly believe there should be an entirely different word created to describe divorce when children are involved. It is just a completely different beast than navigating a split when there are no shared offspring. At the very least I'm gonna need it to come with an asterisk: divorced*. Let it be known far and wide that this particular split came with a special set of circumstances.

I mentioned this complaint to my ex, and she said divorce with kids should be called, "Psych!"

As in, "You thought you were getting rid of me, didn't you? Psych!"

I think she's on the right track.

A Divorce Squad member said, "I think of my ex as a face tattoo I got when I was drunk in my twenties. If we hadn't had kids together, she could have simply been an unfortunate back tattoo I got, embarrassing and ill advised, but I wouldn't see it often or think about it much. But no, since we had kids, my ex is a face tattoo. A constant reminder of the worst mistake I've ever made."

What a poetic way to describe divorce with kids. Feel free to meme it.

As you work your way through your divorce, it may take a while for the realities of co-parenting to fully expose themselves. In the beginning, co-parenting is just another thing you are dealing with in your life explosion. But as time passes, most of the dramas of your divorce have a way of working themselves out. You come out the other side as a new person, with a whole new life. And that life is a good one.

It is at that point that having to collaborate with your ex can really start to stand out as the one part of your new life that isn't feeling particularly worked out. One might even say it feels a bit like an unfortunate tattoo in an unfortunate area, in that it feels glaringly out of place in your new life.

But, as I mentioned previously, you have to do this. So let's explore some ways to survive this never-ending group project in the long term.

Lower Your Expectations

Once you've made it through the first months or even years of your co-parenting experiment, you may have big dreams of the two of you starting a podcast called *We Kick Ass at Divorce*. But. We are going to need to lower the expectations a bit here. There are significant reasons the two of you didn't work, and those reasons aren't going to magically disappear simply because you are both making a real effort to co-parent well.

My ex has always been a perpetually late human being. It drove me nuts when we were together, and shockingly enough, it continued to drive me nuts once we split up. In the early days of our split, we had to do our kid exchanges at the school because one of our kids was doing home school and the other was in school (yay pandemics!). Without fail, my ex would be late to every kid exchange. The bell would ring, the kids would get out of school, and she would pull up five to ten minutes later. She wasn't *that* late, but I thought it demonstrated a lack of consideration for my time and our kids' time.

I had spent twelve years having to coordinate my life around what I saw as my ex's inability to manage her time. But I was no longer doing life with her, and I was not willing to continue accepting this bullshit.

Finally, I told her that the next time she was late, I was leaving with the kids, and she could figure out how to get them from me at a different time and place. The very next exchange day she was late. I walked the kids to my car, put them in, and started driving. I ignored my ex trying to get ahold of me, asking me to wait. I drove away from the school but didn't go to my house, which was only a few minutes away. Instead, I decided to run a few errands. She caught up to me eventually and started waving wildly from her car, "What are you DOING?!"

I rolled down my window at a stop light and said, "I'm running some errands. I told you I wasn't waiting for you anymore." And then I took us all on a nice little drive, ending at the post office downtown. She was livid. The kids were confused.

I was trying to teach her a lesson. I was picking a fight and digging in my heels and throwing a fit; I'd dealt with this shit for twelve years, and I was tired of it. She needed to grow up and start being the kind of person who is considerate of other people's time.

But here's the thing. She's not that kind of person. It's never been who she is, and it's never going to be who she is. Me driving our asses all over town was not teaching anyone a lesson; it was making me look like a crazy person, and she immediately wrote me off as such. It was also costing me a lot more than just the five minutes of time that she would have made me wait for her at the school.

I had to lower my expectations for her and leave them low, or I was going to spend the next decade of my life very frustrated. So now, instead of getting upset that she's late, I just expect it. I don't bug her with reminders, I don't get stressed when I'm waiting for her to show up at a kid event, and I get to be pleasantly surprised if she actually shows up on time.

Tardiness is not a huge deal in the scheme of things, and it's hardly the only issue that my ex and I have. But it's a good example of picking your battles and accepting that the person you divorced is probably going to always have the characteristics that led to that divorce. Be honest with yourself and with each other about what your hurdles are going to be as you attempt to do this project together. Yes, it can be frustrating, but you can take comfort in knowing that at the end of the day, the two of you no longer have to go home together. So at least you have that small victory.

Keep It Fair

Parenting your children is the responsibility of you and your ex. End of list. Things can start to get noisy after a divorce, with friends, family, and new partners constantly voicing their opinions about your life. All of those people most likely mean well, but in the end, their votes mean absolutely nothing when it comes to how you and your ex choose to parent your kids together. Do each of you a favor, and ask everyone else to kindly see their way out of the boardroom, leaving just the two of you to hash out the vote.

Another way this plays out is that you really need to make sure that you invite your ex to be involved in all the votes. A lot of us handled most of the parenting matters pre-divorce and are not particularly excited to share the reins after our split. But this is a two-person board of directors, and your ex is entitled to their vote. They no longer just have to go along with whatever you decide is best, and they should be encouraged to have and voice their opinions.

This is a chance for both of you to fully participate in your kids' lives, and it's important that you allow each other the space to show up in an equal way. Sometimes this enthusiasm is short-lived or solely for the purpose of impressing a new partner, but if your ex is trying, for whatever reason, give them the chance to participate for as long as they show up.

Avoid Old Assumptions

In the early days of our split, my ex and I were too quick to rely on each other when either of us needed something covered. I'd call her to help when the kids were sick, she'd call me to take the kids when a scheduling conflict came up. But eventually we both had to learn that we were no longer and should no longer be each other's first call.

We are raising these kids together, and I will always have her back when it comes to that project. But that doesn't automatically pull me into her orbit for all life matters. In the earlier days of our split, I would begrudgingly say yes when she asked for help with whatever spin show had come up. It would rattle me and inconvenience my life while making me resentful—just like it had when we were together. In most of these cases, I convinced myself it was better for the kids if I helped out. When I finally started saying no, it was met with incredulity. But the more I said no, the more she started expecting it, and the less upset she was by it.

I had to get used to her saying no to me as well. After a few times getting frustrated that she wasn't willing to adjust her schedule to help me out with sick kids, I learned that she is no longer the person I call when we are in a bind. And that's okay. We should both be able to say no to each other if we want to without it causing a skirmish.

Marriage requires a lot of compromise and support. You and your ex will have your routines and will be used to being each other's first phone call. It may take a minute before you think to call someone else or you feel comfortable saying no when you are called upon. But it's important that you push past your instincts and force your relationship into its new form. It may take a few tries to get it right, but eventually the boundaries will do wonders for your attempts to build this new relationship in better ways.

Don't Get Confused

Sometimes divorced couples can get so good at co-parenting that they start to wonder if maybe they might be able to make the marriage thing work again. I even know people who have checked in with their exes before agreeing to marry their new partners. They were getting along well with the ex, they were parenting the kids successfully, family get-togethers were running smoothly . . . maybe . . .

No. No maybes.

You had years and years to get your marriage right, and you weren't able to do it. If you are getting along now that is great for everyone, most notably the kids. But take a real look at what you are doing and why it's going well. The #1 reason for your success is most likely this: You are not actually doing life together anymore. You have two separate houses, two separate lives, and two new ways of moving through the world. These new versions of your lives and your selves are working for each of you and making it easier for you to do the parenting gig together.

Don't mess it up by changing the equation!

Lower Your Expectations Even More

As time passes you may eventually get to a point where you have to let go of the hopes you had for what your co-parenting relationship would look like. You may have seen exes who have it all figured out, with seemingly perfect modern families full of holidays, sideline high fives, and delightful group text strings. You and your ex may have even spoken at length about pulling off an exceptional display of teamwork post-split.

But sometimes reality can't quite keep up with best-laid plans. And that's okay.

Divorce will change the shape of your family, and that shape may evolve in ways you weren't expecting. New partners will come on the scene, new lives will be built, and new boundaries will change what everyone is comfortable with.

All of that is okay. Lower your expectations, and keep lowering them if you have to. Give your co-parenting relationship the space it needs to evolve into whatever it is going to be, even if that means letting go of what you really wanted it to be.

DIVORCE SQUAD

Co-Parenting for the Long Haul

"Our divorce was awful and messy. But we are great co-parents now. People always think we are still married, because we sit together at sports stuff and we get along so well. We even do Christmas morning together. It's all what is best for the kids, and I just had to put everything else to the side and focus on them."

....

"I was so grateful when he got a long-term girlfriend. At first I could tell that he was only putting on a show for her, trying to play the role of the good dad. But eventually, the longer they stayed together, he kept it up. I think his girlfriend called him out when he was being a shit dad and he wanted to keep her happy, so slowly he became a better father to our son."

....

"It's been twelve years since I left him, and he still won't look me in the eye or communicate with me. It makes co-parenting impossible and it's so hard on the kids."

....

"A big part of our success is that we had to reset what we'd hoped our co-parenting would look like. We'd had a really idealized vision for how things would go, and we just weren't able to pull that off in the early years. We had to adjust our expectations and allow each other more space to build new lives. As the years went on, things naturally got better, because we didn't try to force anything early on."

FUCK YOU, YOU FUCKING FUCK (A TIME FOR JOURNALING)
The Characteristics

One of the biggest mindfucks of divorce with kids is when you realize how much your children remind you of your ex. The similarities can range from simple mannerisms to enraging personality traits, and they can really complicate your post-divorce attempts at Zen. You thought you got rid of this person, and lookee here, there is a mini version of them still arguing with you at the dinner table. That's fun.

This issue can swing from annoying to concerning, depending on the traits you see in your children. You are simply going to have to accept most of the annoying similarities as the cost of doing business with your ex. For the more troubling characteristics, it's probably best to involve a therapist, instead of trying to talk your kid out of being like their other parent.

In either case, a little rage journaling never hurt anyone.

The Ways You Continue to Annoy Me via Our Children

Parenting a child who reminds you of your ex can be a whole bowl of frustration. Here's your time to jot down the annoying inheritance and also try to brainstorm ways you might be able to curb the more concerning behaviors or habits. And maybe send your ex the bill for the therapist both you and your kids are going to need to really get to the bottom of these issues.

FUCK YOU FOR GIVING OUR KID THIS CHARACTERISTIC

_____

_____

_____

_____

_____

WAYS I TRY TO COUNTER THIS CHARACTERISTIC

_____

_____

_____

_____

_____

FUCK YOU FOR GIVING OUR KID THIS CHARACTERISTIC

_____

_____

_____

_____

_____

WAYS I TRY TO COUNTER THIS CHARACTERISTIC

_____

_____

_____

_____

_____

I ACKNOWLEDGE THAT MAYBE PERHAPS I MIGHT HAVE GIVEN THE CHILD(REN) ONE OR PERHAPS TWO NOT-SO-GREAT CHARACTERISTICS TOO

_____

_____

_____

_____

_____

WAYS I TRY TO COUNTER THESE CHARACTERISTICS

_____

_____

_____

_____

19

Learning Curve

(figuring out how to do all the stuff your partner used to handle in the relationship)

I am a relatively intelligent human being who has been able to successfully navigate adulthood up until this point in my life. But after my split, I stood for hours trying to figure out the logistics of my ridiculously complicated sprinkler system. Grass was turning brown, drip systems were gushing instead of dripping, and there I was turning nozzles and chasing the sound of water all over my front and backyard. More than one neighbor expressed concern as I stood in the street outside my house, messing with the sprinkler app on my phone and cussing at the grass.

During our marriage I took care of the inside of the house and most of the kid matters, and my ex was responsible for the outside of the house and our complicated financial life. Taking over her share of the responsibilities was daunting, to say the least. Mostly because I wasn't exactly left with a handy list of what she used to do, so I was flying a bit blind.

First, I had to get my arms around all the different bills that needed to be paid each month, with passwords and auto-pays and due dates strewn all over the place. Luckily for me, I'm a pro at Excel and was able to get everything color coded and organized rather quickly. For the more intricate tax matters, I promptly hired a CPA, because I knew the IRS probably wouldn't accept my color-coded spreadsheet in lieu of a tax return.

The outside of the house was a different matter, entirely. It seemed like every day something else went wrong in the backyard, to the point where it felt like every time I stepped outside, I ended up having to throw money at some new issue. The sprinklers weren't working, the spa broke, lighting went haywire, the plants were dying, and there was a massive unidentified leak happening *somewhere*. The Lord was testing me, and I did not feel like I was passing the exam.

In the very beginning, when you are still raw from the life explosion, these new tasks can start to feel like the sprinkler head that broke the camel's back. They are just ONE MORE THING you have to do, during a time when you are SO FUCK-ING DONE WITH EVERYTHING.

Looking back on those frustrating days, I realize they really weren't that big of a deal in the long run. The new tasks were added to my list, and over time they slowly just became part of my day-to-day duties. And I promise it will be the same for you eventually as well. But until that time, I have some advice on how to handle your new learning curves.

How to Do the Things

Evaluate

The first step to figuring out what new tasks are going to be added to your to-do list is to take a truthful look at what your partner used to contribute to the management of your household. Maybe they did the bills or mowed the lawn or took out the trash or cooked a majority of the meals. Write it all down. Try to think really hard about all the things they might have done that you weren't even aware of. Like changing the air filters or the batteries in the smoke detectors. (They also probably contributed in less helpful ways, such as piling dishes to the ceiling or being unaware that your laundry room even existed. Put those on the list too, lest you start becoming nostalgic.)

Tackle It

Now it's time to roll up your sleeves and get some shit done. Yes, these tasks may be way outside of your wheelhouse, but you are a grown-ass person and you can handle your business. Maybe your ex used to manage the bills, so it's time for you to become friendly with Microsoft Excel. Maybe they did a lot of cooking, so start channeling your inner Martha. Maybe they used to clean the rain gutters, so . . . no. Don't start cleaning rain gutters, let's not get out of hand.

Which leads us to . . .

Know Your Limits

Look, you are a grown-ass person, yes, but let's not get ridiculous here. One of the biggest favors I have done for myself in my old age is admitting that I cannot do ALL THE THINGS. Or, more accurately, I do not have the time or inclination to do ALL THE THINGS. You have gone from a partnership to a solo operation, and it just might not be feasible or efficient to take on everything your ex used to do.

In my case, I happened to divorce my CPA, which turned out to be quite unfortunate at tax time. My ex said to me, "Your return isn't that complicated, you can totally do it yourself." And she was not wrong. If I sat down and concentrated and did a little research and math . . . yes, I *could* do my taxes myself. But taxes feel like a pretty important thing, where accuracy and aptitude are rather large requirements. So I said to her, "Yeah, I'm a writer and a designer . . . I'm not doing my taxes."

Get Good at Asking for Help

You are just one grown-ass person. And sometimes grown-ass people need a little help. Asking for help doesn't make you weak or pathetic; it makes you human. And other humans are usually happy to help, especially if that help involves doing something they can do well. If there is a particular task that is not quite your forte, find a friend who is good at said task and ask them to help you. They don't need to do the task for you indefinitely; you just need a little guidance on how to get the thing done. They can be For Dummies guide come to life, just for your education.

After my split I enlisted the help of a friend in the neighborhood and assigned him the title of My Dude. I would call on him for any and all Dude tasks that needed to be accomplished. Some he just flat-out did for me, but others he walked me through so that I could do them myself in the future. For instance, he told me how to change my weirdly complicated air filters and promised to call 911 in fifteen minutes if I didn't call him back. Because ladders can be tricky.

(Please note that I understand it is extremely sexist to assume some tasks can only be done by a Dude. I obviously don't believe that, since most of my Dude tasks were previously done by my female partner. There are just some things that have been stereotypically classified as the responsibilities that dudes favor, and I happened to have a dude willing to help me with them. I would have gladly accepted that help from any gender, so make sure you cast your net wide when you are looking for assistance.)

Outsource

At a certain point, you must also be willing to admit that there are some things you cannot do and will not be doing ever. And there is no friend who can or should take over the permanent handling of these things. That is when we get to the outsourcing portion of our program. Personally, I got to this portion rather quickly.

I added sprinkler guys, landscape guys, pool guys, and electricians to my list of contacts and did not hesitate to call them when things went sideways. At Christmastime I hired a dude to hang the lights on my house, because as I mentioned, ladders can be tricky.

The biggest help I found was a local handyman who took over for my friend and became My Dude for Hire. After a while I felt bad constantly asking my friend to do Dude Things for me, and I was lucky enough to find an honest handyman who was available. This guy could do anything and everything I needed around the house. I'd make a list that included tasks like hanging heavy pictures and shelves, installing ceiling fans and shower heads, and even assembling a huge ping pong table. As soon as the Dude List had a few items on it, I would reach out to My Dude for Hire, and he'd take care of the things.

Could I have feasibly done all of these things myself? Yes. But life is short and my patience is thin. I could have spent hours doing these things, with regular face-plants over their many learning curves. Or I could pay My Dude for Hire to do them while I focused my energies on much more rewarding tasks that did not involve ladders or the screaming of profanity-laced frustrations. I recommend you evaluate the risk/reward for each of your required tasks and outsource as many as you need to keep yourself sane.

Energy Delegation

The internet exists to give us an abundance of information about all the shit we do not know. Take advantage of that to make a plan of attack for your new duties. Just because you haven't done a particular task before doesn't mean you can't figure out how to do it well.

But on the other hand, you are only one person, and kicking ass at every single thing can get a little exhausting. When you've reached your mastery limit, just go ahead and throw some money at it.

Make some decisions below about how you plan to tackle all the things:

Budgeting/Bills

☐ I got this, easy peasy

☐ Ask the interwebs

- ☐ YouTube it!
- ☐ Phone a friend
- ☐ Throw money at it

Grocery Shopping / Cooking

- ☐ Easy peasy
- ☐ Ask the interwebs
- ☐ YouTube it!
- ☐ Phone a friend
- ☐ Throw money at it

Childcare / Kids Stuff

- ☐ Easy peasy
- ☐ Ask the interwebs
- ☐ YouTube it!
- ☐ Phone a friend
- ☐ Throw money at it

Yardwork

- ☐ Easy peasy
- ☐ Ask the interwebs
- ☐ YouTube it!
- ☐ Phone a friend
- ☐ Throw money at it

Housework

- ☐ Easy peasy
- ☐ Ask the interwebs
- ☐ YouTube it!

☐ Phone a friend
☐ Throw money at it

Home Repairs
☐ Easy peasy
☐ Ask the interwebs
☐ YouTube it!
☐ Phone a friend
☐ Throw money at it

Random Hassle: _____
☐ Easy peasy
☐ Ask the interwebs
☐ YouTube it!
☐ Phone a friend
☐ Throw money at it

Thing I Don't Want to Do: _____
☐ Easy peasy
☐ Ask the interwebs
☐ YouTube it!
☐ Phone a friend
☐ Throw money at it

Annoying New Responsibility: _____
☐ Easy peasy
☐ Ask the interwebs
☐ YouTube it!
☐ Phone a friend
☐ Throw money at it

DIVORCE SQUAD

Old Dog, New Tricks

"He still handles the drip system. I just don't want to learn. I had asked him to help me on the Christmas lights, and he was being an ass so I just did it myself to spite him. The most frustrating has been the budget because I suck at that. Trying to remember to make sure ALL of the bills are paid is a lot for my brain."

....

"Well, I cook more. I was a decent cook before, but I didn't love the responsibility of cooking all of the time. Now I have embraced it and I really enjoy it. I have about nine or ten new recipes I'm experimenting with."

....

"There were definitely things around the house that my ex used to do, and I had to learn how to do those things. But, honestly, not having to clean up after my ex or manage their life every day really did free up a lot of time to do other things!"

....

"The kid stuff was easy. I always did everything anyways, so that wasn't a big deal. But when other things go wrong, I have to ask for help to get them fixed, and I'm not really good at asking for help."

20

Letting Go

(the art of breathing out the bullshit)

I'm a type A hypervigilant perfectionist who is very good at being very good. I'm very not good with imperfections or feeling out of control. Parenthood did a number on these personality traits because never did I strive to be more perfect, and never did I fall so incredibly short. Every. Single. Day.

Creating little humans from scratch and being responsible for their survival pushed my hypervigilance into overdrive. I wore worry like a (very heavy, very uncomfortable) scarf around my neck. I worried about their health, I worried that I wasn't good enough, I worried that everything I was doing or wasn't doing was somehow inflicting permanent damage upon the children. I was a ton of fun, let me tell you.

Over time, I had to let go of perfectionism because it was simply no longer an option when it came to managing a life that included kids and a career and a partnership. I had to give us all a lot of grace and accept that perfect was off the menu for the indefinite future. It was a bit liberating, to be honest. I leaned into the mess and the chaos and made peace with all the beauty that can be found in the imperfections of parenting. Where I used to stress, I would now just shrug. "It is what it is" became my mantra of mediocrity.

But. I never did stop worrying. Over time it wound around into the pit of my belly, always there, always reminding me of exactly how fragile a heart is when it's walking around outside of your body.

With that grasp on sanity firmly in place, I set off on the task of navigating a post-divorce world that included being away from my kids 50 percent of the time. This setup did wonders for the hypervigilance, if you were wondering.

The worry intensified, not because Elizabeth was a bad mom, but because my heart was now not only walking around outside of my body; it was walking around well outside of my reach half the time.

As the worry intensified, so did the perfectionism. I was feeling out of control, so I tried to wrangle the situation into order by implementing unrealistic expectations on all of us. We were all navigating a completely new normal, and instead of giving us grace, I dug in my heels and demanded everything run exactly as I wanted it to.

Of course, this backfired spectacularly. Because perfection is not really an option in the immediate aftermath of a divorce. There were learning curves for all of us, and all of our curves were big on bumps. Instead of being patient with these bumps, I grew frustrated.

This frustration went on for months and months. For months and months I banged my head against the immovable wall of our new family dynamics. The worry wound heavier and heavier in my gut, until I finally had to acknowledge that I couldn't spend the next decade of my kids' lives trying to hold on to control I was never going to have again.

I had to let go.

That sounds simple in theory. Just let go. Just release all the fear and anxiety and expectation, and everything will be immeasurably better for everyone. It's an easy enough concept to comprehend but much more difficult to execute.

Part of the difficulty stemmed from the fact that there were so many different areas of this new life that were proving to be frustrating. How on earth would I let go of every one of them every single day?

The answer was . . . I had to let go of every one of them every single day. There was no snap of the finger, there was no quick fix. There was only choosing every single day, sometimes multiple times a day. To. Just. Let. Go.

Instead of getting frustrated, I would stop, close my eyes, and take a deep breath. I would breathe in slowly, intentionally, and then I would breathe out all the bullshit. Some days I did this so often I nearly hyperventilated, but over time it got easier. Just like I had at the beginning of parenthood, I leaned back into the shrug. "It is what it is" made a reappearance in my vocabulary, less as an acceptance of mediocrity and more as just an overall acceptance of the new reality I created by leaving my marriage.

All of this was hardly an overnight fix, and I'd be lying if I said the bullshit doesn't still take up a pretty powerful residency now and again. But if you are looking to get started on your own journey to letting go, let me share with you a few ways I got good at breathing out the bullshit.

Breathe In, Breathe Out

Breathe In: The Bullshittery

I divorced my ex, but then in a cruel twist of fate, I was still required to collaborate with her on our very important parenting project. And—you're going to be shocked when I tell you this— she continued to be a very frustrating person post-divorce. I grew increasingly frazzled because didn't I blow up my entire life to get away from this bullshittery?

I would constantly point out where she was failing, I'd repeatedly get upset when I was affected by her scattered way of doing life, I'd pull my hair out imagining the next decade of co-parenting with this impossible human.

Breathe Out: Control What You Can

And then. Something clicked

She. Was. Not. Going. To. Change. I could spend the next decade being frustrated by that fact, or I could figure out what part of the equation I actually had control over. And that part was me. I could stop announcing all the ways she was failing, I could refuse to engage in her chaos, I could let go of expectations that would never, ever be met. I couldn't change her, but I could alter my reactions to her.

It was very freeing to completely abandon hope of another person changing and instead concentrate solely on changing myself. I think by making it an inside job, I effectively regained a little bit of control over a situation that had been spinning outside of my grasp for quite some time.

One of the biggest gifts you can give yourself in your healing from divorce is getting to a place where you finally accept that the person you divorced is probably going to keep being the person you divorced. They may never change, but you can change whether or not you allow them access to your nervous system. This one will take a while to really pull off, and you may never feel like you completely succeed, because your kids are involved, but it's definitely the best way to find peace in a potentially erratic time.

Breathe In: The Different Kid Rules

One of the most frustrating aspects of co-parenting in two separate houses is how different the parenting can look in each home. When we were together, my ex and I would collaborate on all parenting matters. Even when we disagreed, there would be a discussion and eventually one accepted plan of attack.

This collaboration ended when our marriage did. As a person who was used to having a say in all matters involving my kids . . . it was very difficult to accept the idea that I had no control over how they were parented 50 percent of the time.

Breathe Out: The Kids Are Alright

But. My ex loves our kids more than anything on the planet. When they are at her house, I know that they are happy and healthy and adored. This is not the case for all divorced couples, and I've learned to find peace in knowing that our kids have two safe homes that they love.

If you are in a situation where you are frustrated by what is happening at your ex's house, you have to decide whether it's worth your energy to engage with your ex about it. If it simply comes down to different rules or lax discipline, it's probably not worth the argument. But if there are really concerning things happening at your kids' other house, then I do not recommend simply making peace with it. Push back, file requests with the court, fight for the kids to have two safe homes that they can love.

And then breathe out, knowing that you are always willing to fight for the things that matter, while letting the smaller stuff go.

Breathe In: The New People

When two people split up, they not only stop doing life together; they actively start building lives separate from each other. This is just the natural progression of things, but it doesn't make it any easier to accept a whole new cast of characters entering your kids' lives.

Breathe Out: Trust

There is no simple answer to this one, especially if you are not in a good place with your ex. Ultimately, you have to simply trust that your co-parent is going to make choices that are in the best interest of your kids, but we all know that is not a given for every divorced couple.

If you aren't able to trust your ex to make good choices about who they bring into the kids' lives, then you'll have to shift your focus over to the kids themselves. Keep an open line of communication with your children, and make sure they know it is always safe to tell you about anything that is making them uncomfortable at either house, yours included. The tried and true Car Time Talk is a great place to start these conversations and build trust with your offspring. Something about you in the driver's seat and the kids in the backseat allows for more honest conversations than might occur during a formal face-to-face sit-down.

Start these conversations early and often, so that if and when there is something serious to talk about, the lines of communication are already open.

Breathe In: The Injustice

Divorce is the process of completely blowing up a life. I'm sure there are other ways to describe it, and I'm sure some of those lives really needed to be blown up, but that doesn't change the fact that an explosion has taken place and that the entire point of the explosion was to blow one life into two.

Odds are, when one thing is being broken into two, both sides are going to end up feeling like they are left with less than they deserve. This can lead to resentment and a festering sense that a great injustice has been done to you via your divorce proceedings.

Breathe Out: It's Over

At a certain point you have to cut your losses and be done. With all of it. With the shitty relationship, with the shitty divorce, with all the shit. Let go of the festering and chalk the whole thing up to "Well, that sucked." And leave it back where it belongs, in the past; don't carry it into the present or future with you. Let it be over.

Breathe In: The Competition

Here's the thing with perfectionists, we tend to be a little competitive. Because striving to be really, really good at everything leads us to really, really want to win at *all the things*. It also leads us to great rage in the face of loss or even perceived inadequacies. (We are a super fun bunch to invite to game night.)

After a breakup it's natural to keep a bit of a scorecard with your ex. You are expecting them to fail dramatically in all aspects of their lives without you, and anything less is infuriating. This scorecard can turn into a real competition to see who "wins" post-divorce. Who is handling their finances best, who is moving on to a new relationship first, who is being the better parent, who is having the best post-divorce glow-up. Of course this competition is a complete waste of time and energy, but logic is not a huge factor in divorce emotions.

Breathe Out: You Do You

Competing against what you know about anyone else's life is always going to be a futile task. It's like following someone on Instagram and honestly believing that their posted photos encompass their entire life when, in reality, Instagram actually represents a very carefully curated version of it. You are essentially comparing a well-lit, well-staged, possibly Photoshopped Instagram image to the photo of your left nostril that you accidently took when trying to use the calculator app on your phone. It ain't apples to apples, is what I'm saying. And that same thing can happen when you start comparing your life to whatever you think is happening in your ex's life.

In my case, I jumped into a new relationship way too early post-divorce, partly because I was subconsciously trying to keep up with my ex. She found someone and I should too, right? Or else I would be losing, and I'm not a fan of losing. But as it turned out, the person who really ended up losing was the poor soul who had to be in a relationship with my broken ass way before I should have been allowed in public.

When I look back on that time, I feel like my ex was running a sprint and I really needed to run a marathon. Maybe her healing required another person, but my healing required a lot of work on my own. Neither of our journeys was better than the other, but it was stupid of me to try to alter mine to match hers.

When my new relationship imploded, I took it as a loss, but in the end, it was exactly what was necessary to get me where I needed to go. Everyone's life ebbs and flows, times are good and bad, victories and defeats get woven together like a tapestry over the years.

Your journey after your divorce may not look the same as your ex's, but it's pointless to compare your mile markers to theirs. Because guess what? They aren't headed where you are headed. Your divorce was a fork in the road. Don't waste time looking back.

You have places to go.

FUCK YOU, YOU FUCKING FUCK (A TIME FOR JOURNALING)
Breathing Out the Bullshit

It can be very difficult to fully reach a post-divorce Zen state when you are constantly having to deal with your ex's bullshittery. It's like trying to meditate while someone stands in front of you playing reggaeton on a megaphone. It can kill the vibe you are going for, to say the least. But at a certain point, you have to figure out a way to tune out the noise and concentrate only on the things that really matter.

Unfortunately, this is not a quick, one-time fix. It will be a skill that may be called upon daily, especially in the early days of your co-parenting project. But the good news is, you'll have plenty of opportunities to practice getting it right! You'll be an expert in no time at all.

To help you on your road to bullshit immunity, jump over to your journal to hash out a plan of attack for each of your ex's most common megaphone annoyances. Take a deep breath and jot down their ridiculousness, going into detail about why it drives you insane (breathe in). Then slowly release that breath and formulate a plan for letting the ridiculousness bounce right off you (breathe out).

Imagine you are like Wonder Woman wielding her magic bracelets to repel attacks. If you need to also involve a headband and a lasso, so be it. Everyone's journey to inner peace requires different tools.

BREATHE IN _____

_____

_____

_____

_____

BREATHE OUT _____

_____

_____

_____

_____

BREATHE IN _____

_____

_____

_____

_____

BREATHE OUT _____

_____

_____

_____

_____

21

Forgiveness

(how to forgive yourself [and your ex]
for all the things that went wrong)

I put this chapter at the end of the book, because I'm fully aware that you probably won't be ready to read it for quite some time. And that's okay. I'm just going to leave it right here for you to pick up when you are ready.

In Chapter 5, "The Seven Stages of Divorce," I said that the last stage of this mess is the shrug, moving into a state of indifference about the whole thing. And I still believe the shrug is where you will ultimately end up, but I also think somewhere around the All the Therapy stage, you will really need to look into what it means to forgive. In fact, it was actually my own therapist who gave me the assignment to "think about what forgiveness looks like to you."

I thought about it a lot, because I take my therapy homework very seriously. I rolled it around and around in my head for days on end, trying to figure out what forgiveness would look like but mostly trying to figure out what forgiveness would feel like. What I landed on was the absence of a feeling, specifically the absence of the feeling I had been carrying around with me for as long as I could remember. The feeling was a mix of resentment and sorrow and rage and regret. It sat in the pit of my gut and had been rumbling like a steady hum for years.

I realized that forgiveness would mean the silencing of that rumbling, a stillness. But knowing what forgiveness would feel like still offered me very little in the way of a road map. The homework felt incomplete.

Then I remembered a quote about forgiveness that I have leaned on repeatedly throughout my life, "Forgiveness is letting go of the hope that the past could be different." When that quote popped into my head, it brought with it a path forward that I had been unable to see for a very long time.

In my case, the person I had to forgive was myself. And I was not particularly interested in letting myself off the hook easily. I was carrying with me a deep anger over the way I had allowed my life to go and for the choices I had made that created a world in which I only had my kids 50 percent of the time. A world where I would have to co-parent with a person I had no interest in speaking to ever again. How had I let this happen?

When I turned thirty years old, I made a promise to myself to start going on more second dates. I had a history of dismissing people very quickly after only one date, and I wanted to open myself up a bit more. I met Elizabeth a few months after my thirtieth birthday. On the drive home from our first date I said, out loud, to myself, "She might be cool if she calmed down."

I knew in my gut from Date #1 that her energy was too much for my nervous system, and yet I stuck with my promise to myself to go on more second dates. We connected in a lot of different ways, wanted a lot of the same things, and we made a lot of sense on paper. It was the time in both of our lives when we were looking to settle down and have kids, so the dates kept happening.

We were complete opposites personality-wise, but Paula Abdul and MC Skat Kat had told me that opposites attract, so I went with it. Turns out Paula and Skat led me very, very astray, which is probably to be expected from a couple made up of one human and one animated cat wearing overalls.

Over time we built a huge life together and made a lot of our dreams come true. But none of that ever overcame the fact that my nervous system knew we weren't a good fit. In fact, the more dreams we conquered and the bigger our life got, the more glaring it became that our relationship was the only thing not working.

Eventually I could no longer ignore the fact that doing all this with the wrong person was completely emptying out my soul. And filling it with all that resentment and sorrow and rage and regret. Finally, I just gave up. On her, on us, on our big life together. And we both deserved so much better than a relationship that was given up on.

So then. How could I go about forgiving myself for all of that pain? How could I start to let go of the anger I had toward myself for creating this broken life brick by wavering brick?

A big part of forgiving myself was fully accepting the role I played in my failed relationship.

Yes, Elizabeth and I were opposite humans, and yes, our differences made partnership very difficult. But Elizabeth never deserved to be with a person who thought completely shutting down and becoming ice cold was a suitable reaction to relationship issues. She deserved someone who was able to articulate their hurt, instead of piling it up as a wall between the two of us, regularly hurling nastiness from behind that wall as a way of keeping her at a distance.

After I acknowledged the role I played in the breakup, I spent a long time in the anger portion of the program. Anger at myself, anger at my ex, anger at the damn universe for ever putting us in each other's paths. I had plenty of anger to go around. Focusing that anger on immovable facts was my favorite pastime. The humming of resentment and sorrow and rage and regret got louder and louder in my gut.

Until finally, "Forgiveness is letting go of the hope that the past could be different."

I went into great detail about my letting go journey in Chapter 20, "Letting Go," and it took all those details to get me to a place where I was actually able to let go of the immovable facts of the past and begin to forgive both of us for things that couldn't be changed.

Many of the people in my Divorce Squad had divorce experiences that were a lot different from mine. They were cheated on, they had to navigate their ex's mental illness, they were blindsided by a sudden divorce demand that destroyed their life. The rage they felt post-divorce was targeted specifically at their ex and rightfully so. And you may be in the same spot.

My tale of simply picking the wrong person to do life with may sound almost quaint compared to the shit show of your relationship destruction. The idea of merely "letting go of the hope that the past could be different" might not feel like an option anytime soon. And that's okay. That's why this chapter is at the end of the book; it's most likely going to be one of the very last things you are able to do, if you are ever able to do it.

But I do want to plant the seed.

It's simple to think of forgiveness in divorce as only the process of absolving your ex, and that is definitely a requirement for most breakups. But marriage is a two-person job, and I think it's lazy to place 100 percent of the blame on only one participant's shoulders. Relationships are complex and evolving and nuanced. The way they end rarely encompasses all the ways they went wrong over the course of things.

Where did things go wrong? What role did you play in them going wrong? What did you ignore or overlook or simply allow when you knew they weren't quite right? How could you have demanded something better, for yourself and for your partnership?

This isn't about beating yourself up; it's about trying to find some lessons in the rubble, instead of just blame. You are going to rebuild again someday, so it's worth really owning what you could do better the next time around (and no, "Don't marry an asshole" can't be the only lesson you learn).

Buddhists believe there are no mistakes, only lessons. I'm pretty sure that's just something we tell ourselves to feel better about our mistakes, but it's healthier than the alternative, so let's go with the Buddhists on this one. The past can't be different, but the future can look a whole lot better if we take the lessons and leave the anger.

One of my Divorce Squad went through a divorce after his marriage slowly died on the vine. I asked him if he regretted all the years he spent with his ex. He quickly answered, "No. We are all the sum total of our lives and we have to let shit go."

In time, I hope we can all land on this level of acceptance about the journey that led us to where we are right now and what that journey can teach us about where we are headed. Do yourself a favor and forgive the things that can't be different, and instead focus on avoiding the same bullshit in the future. It's your very own serenity prayer of sorts, with profanity thrown in to keep you interested in the process.

DIVORCE SQUAD

Forgiveness

"I feel like I made a conscious effort to forgive him . . . for the kids. Like it wasn't an option. We had kids to raise . . . and that was our job, regardless of what had happened. It was a business decision.

"As for forgiving myself. . . . I just tried to give myself grace and only control what I could. I definitely feel like I overdo things because I'm trying to make up for being a divorced family. That still hasn't gone away."

....

"If forgiveness comes, it's just time. Some of it's spiritual. And it may never truly come for many of us. That is just real life."

....

"The thing that has been hardest for me in the divorce has been things that are true, like this is a fact. And I'm like, 'That fact fucking sucks!' I'm so mad and it's so unchangeable. As time has passed that's something that I feel like I'm handling better. I now see a fact and instead of being angry about it I just accept it and forgive it. That was my healing journey though."

22

New You

*(follow the midlife crisis checklist
for best results)*

I have repeatedly described divorce as a "life explosion" in this book. On the whole, explosions are seen as a less than appealing event. And they are. Exploding a whole life is scary and daunting and rattling. But an explosion can also be uniquely transformative. How often in life do you have the opportunity to completely reset who you are, where you are headed, and what your ab muscles look like? Not often. Ab muscles are elusive bastards.

Way back in my twenties, my young little heart was broken in a spectacular fashion. And, because I was in my twenties, this broken heart absolutely destroyed me and my life for quite some time. But when I look back at every good thing I've accomplished since that time, I can trace almost all of them back to that broken heart, to that life explosion. At the time the hurt felt endless and insurmountable, but in hindsight I see that it was a blip, a sharp right turn that led me to places I never would have ventured otherwise.

When my marriage exploded, I was in my forties and a much older and wiser version of myself. As such I knew that my divorce would eventually be just a sharp right turn too, and the best way to get around that corner was to do whatever I could to keeping moving forward, instead of rolling around in the mess for too long. Life explosions provide the unique opportunity to rebuild in better ways, and I was looking forward to what the new version of me would look like. Especially since I barely recognized anything about the current version of myself.

(I know that you might still be firmly rooted in your mess and rebuilding may be on hold while you fully examine your rage and snack food proclivities. That's okay too. You do you. And come back here when you are ready.)

My New Me journey was a bit more literal than most, because I literally added some new parts to my body during the process. As I mentioned previously, I have really bad hearing that has gotten progressively worse throughout my life. My right ear went totally deaf during my pregnancies, and my left ear was nearly useless as well, even with a hearing aid. In the years leading up to my divorce, I was slowly going completely deaf.

It's hard to accurately describe what it's like to have the world start to go silent around you. I had to primarily read lips to understand what was being said, which was fine one on one but started to fail me in any situation with multiple people. Parties were exhausting and overwhelming. The telephone was torture. COVID masks made communication impossible. Rather than putting myself in social situations, I slowly started to isolate from the world, because that was an easier option. I passed up on professional opportunities that would have required me to attend conferences or meetings, neither of which I could functionally do. I had trouble understanding my children when they spoke.

Conveniently enough, my marriage was also slowly dying at the same time my hearing was marching toward oblivion. What an exciting time for me both mentally and physically! Between my unhappiness and my deafness, I isolated more and more, and my world got smaller and smaller.

A cochlear implant was my last best hope to avoid going completely deaf. The implant bypassed my dead ear and went straight to my auditory nerve, restoring my ability to hear. It was nothing short of a miracle that a simple outpatient surgery completely restored one of my senses.

I had the surgery two weeks after I left Elizabeth.

And so.

I'd spent the past twelve years slowly dying in a bad relationship and slowly having the world fade away as I went deaf. In the matter of a few weeks, I came back to life. I was in a new home with a new ear, and I was ready to roll.

But what exactly was I supposed to do?

I had lost 50 percent of my days with the kids, which freed up a lot of "me time." But I had been raising two children for a decade, so I hadn't had me time in quite a long while. Like every other parent, I'd spent the previous years lamenting all the things I could accomplish if *only I had the time*. Now I had the time, but I also had no idea what the hell to do with myself.

I reached out to another divorced woman who was on roughly the same timeline as me, hoping she might have some ideas. She did not disappoint: "I pass the time by picking up new and increasingly outlandish hobbies. It began with French lessons (which seems useful) and has now run the gamut—sailing, golf, horseback riding, acupuncture, therapy (is that a hobby?), tarot card reading, et cetera."

This woman's to-do list sounded very similar to a solid mid-life crisis, and that sounded like a solid plan of attack to me. I started out my midlife crisis journey in a spectacular fashion, by buying a ridiculous car. I'd gotten our minivan in the split, and a mom-mobile was just not going to work as I undertook my New Me transformation. No one has ever had a successful midlife crisis in a minivan, I promise you that.

I began looking at oversized SUVs, because this was not the time for sensible choices. I ended up buying a gigantic cherry-red Chevy Tahoe. It was already huge, but mine had oversized tires that made it impossible to fit into my garage without re-moving the roof racks first. My tiny ass driving around in that boat of a car was basically making it known to all of humanity that I was in the middle of a major life transition. Keep your distance, everyone.

I began dating quite a bit (see Chapter 15, "Belly Flopping Into the Dating Pool") but couldn't quite embrace the stereo-typical dating of younger women. I've never really understood that inclination. I did, however, try to be a little less uptight in other areas of my life. I'd never been much of a drinker, so I started drinking wine with my friends. Turns out I'm a lot of fun when I drink wine. Also turns out I have no tolerance and am a very cheap date.

I also experimented with weed gummies. I'd smoked pot maybe five times in my life, but gummies were a different ex-perience. First of all, they don't hit you right away like inhaled marijuana does. So, I ate a gummy and waited. And waited. Then I ate more gummies. I didn't really feel like it had af-fected me at all. Until I was DoorDashing mini tacos, French fries, and a milkshake at midnight. I was stuffing all of these items into my mouth, giggling about who knows what, and my friend said, "Sweetie, you're stoned." Then I giggled and ate some more. Two thumbs up for weed gummies.

In an effort to expand beyond ill-advised purchases and deep-fried tacos, I asked my friends for some midlife crisis ideas. Their suggestions really set me up for quite a few adventures. One of my first stops on the road to self-discovery was a place called a "smash room." And, well, as the name suggests, it was a room where people go and smash things. The success of this business model seems to suggest that perhaps I'm not the only one who harbors a bit of pent-up aggression.

My friend and I arrived at the smash room and put on protective glasses, a helmet, and some gloves. Then we proceeded to beat the shit out of all sorts of random items. Beer bottles, dishes, electronics, and a windshield. Destruction proved to be very therapeutic, if not a tiny bit dangerous. I found glass in my shoe two days later.

On the flip side of that rage, I had several friends recommend various ways to balance my chi. Reiki was suggested, so I decided to try it out. Reiki is a type of energy healing where the practitioner helps their patient unblock energy so that it can flow freely through the body. This healing usually takes place in person, with the reiki practitioner standing over a patient's body, moving the energy Ouija-board-style without touching the patient. But because of COVID my energy had to be unblocked over the phone. I was skeptical.

My reiki lady told me to lie down on my bed, and then she proceeded to do her energy thing via speakerphone, "I feel like you are carrying your mother in your shoulder."

"My mother? In my shoulder?"

"Yes."

"Okay, I guess move her out of there?"

"I will try."

And that was about how reiki went.

My visit to the tarot card lady went a little bit better than reiki, mostly because she didn't find my mother hanging out in any part of my body. She flipped over all my cards, told me that everything was going to be okay, and I went ahead and chose to believe her. Four stars.

Next, I tried meditation. How could I fail at that? All I had to do was sit still with my eyes closed and clear my mind. Turns out I was only good at two of those things. Nothing cluttered my mind more than sitting still with my eyes closed. I tried meditation in silence and my brain filled the space with an aggressively random stream of consciousness, "It's quiet, I'm quiet, I'm still, I'm a river. STOP. CONCENTRATE. I'm splashing in the river. Remember that time I went swimming in the river with my friends and then we got burgers at that place that most definitely wouldn't have passed a health inspection? BREATHE! STOP GETTING DISTRACTED! The food at those kinds of places is always the best. What am I going to have for dinner? Thai sounds good. NO MORE THOUGHTS! BE CLEAR! I should go to Thailand someday. I wonder how long the flight is . . . " And so on, and so on. Not so much stillness happening.

So then I started doing guided meditations that I found on YouTube. These videos included calming sounds and a soft voice guiding me toward inner peace. This worked better than my silent attempts, but the combination of calming sounds calmed me to sleep a couple of times.

No midlife crisis is complete without a solid body transformation, so I embraced the moving of my body in ways that my lazy ass was not quite prepared for. I started hiking with friends and had to rely heavily on the "why don't we sit down and really breathe in the fresh air and beautiful views for a while" part of mountain climbing.

I headed out for a run every day and quickly remembered why I had stopped running twenty years prior. It turned out that two decades hadn't changed my opinion on running. The pounding of the pavement, the sweating, the miles and miles with only my thoughts to keep me entertained. My chi was not a fan. I tried adding podcasts to the ritual, hoping that they could distract my brain from what was happening to the rest of my body. That didn't work.

I would get home from running a couple of miles and would promptly collapse on the floor. I decided this would be a great time to incorporate some meditation as well. It's important to feel connected to the ground while meditating, and sprawled flat on my back provided quite a bit of that, which was handy. I'd lie there, getting my heart rate and breathing back into a nonemergency-situation range while listening to a guided meditation. Since I was so busy trying not to hyperventilate, my brain didn't have the chance to wander like it usually did during meditation. Success! And so much multitasking!

In a last-ditch effort to trick my mind and body into believing I was physically fit, I took my cousin up on his offer to show me how to box. I went over to his house, put on some gloves, and beat the shit out of a punching bag. And that is where I found my chi. Turns out my chi has some anger issues.

I bought a punching bag and gloves for my house and signed up for a virtual boxing program call FightCamp. FightCamp is kinda like Fight Club, except the first rule of FightCamp is you should most definitely talk to everyone about FightCamp, here is a referral code.

I didn't really know how well I would do with boxing, or if I would stick with it after the novelty wore off in a couple of weeks. But I didn't stop. And for the first time in my life, I had found an exercise routine that I actually enjoyed. The FightCamp boxing workouts ranged from twenty to forty-five minutes, broken up into three-minute rounds. Each round was then broken up into thirty-second or one-minute drills. The instructors were boxers who didn't quite have the sheen that most fitness instructors possess. They reminded me of the dudes and girls I grew up with, instead of the overcaffeinated Mickey Mouse personalities of most fitness instructors. These guys were my style.

The workouts were intense, with my entire body engaged. There was a lot of variety in the punch combinations and strength drills. The coaches were funny, the music was catchy. All of this combined to pull me in and keep me there. I'd finally found something that could distract my mind while my body was getting a workout. And also, it turns out I really, really enjoy hitting the shit out of things.

When I told my therapist about my boxing, she informed me that there is a whole science behind the benefit of bilateral movement. It actually rewires the human brain, and she recommends it a lot to help patients overcome trauma. I nodded, "Yeah, I can see that. But also, I think I really just like hitting the shit out of something."

I've been boxing for two years now, three to five times a week. I'm not sure why it has helped me so much, but I can honestly say that things started to change when I started beating up my heavy bag. I was getting in shape, burning calories, and on my worst days, I had a very handy method to release my frustrations. I've added other workouts to the mix in the past year: occasional running, a fancy stationary bike, some weight lifting. But nothing hits quite the same as lacing up for a few rounds.

A weird thing started to happen the more I raged against my punching bag. Somehow that wailing translated into a calm once I took off my gloves. The chaotic energy and emotions that had been boiling around my mind and body for what seemed liked years slowly started to dial down to a simmer. I finally felt still.

I took a look around me. I was settled in my house, contently single, and my mind was calm. I had reemerged into the world, started saying yes to get-togethers, and began using my new ear to hear people again. I had brought myself back to life.

Once I came out the other side of my midlife crisis, I realized it had taken me quite a long way from where I started, yes, but my final destination wasn't exactly where I had expected to end up. I started being social again, I went from flabby to fit, and my life felt full. But I also traded in my ridiculous tank of a car, I still didn't drink much, and weed gummies were hardly in regular rotation. I was a different person than I was when I started out my crisis, but this new version of me felt quite familiar.

I'd smashed bottles, climbed mountains, meditated poorly, got reiki'd and stoned, threw hundreds of thousands of punches . . . and I didn't end up with a New Me. Instead, I ended up making my way back to just . . . me. I ended up back to the version of me that existed before life and marriage and kids and disability had slowly weighed me down to someone nearly unrecognizable.

My divorce had been an explosion, yes. And there, beneath the rubble, was me. It just took me a while to dig her back out.

Right after my divorce, I didn't feel like doing much of any-thing; I was still numb from the life I had just exploded. Doing anything felt like too big of an ask, because just making it through the day was a pretty big accomplishment. But even-tually I started remembering my last life explosion in my twen-ties. And I remembered that back then things didn't start to get better until I started to move. Sometimes the moving had been literal, sometimes figurative.

This time I knew early on that I needed to move. I needed to stop saying no to life simply because I wasn't particularly fond of my current view. So, instead of saying no, I went ahead and said yes to every damn thing that came my way. I still don't know what the hell my mother was (is?) doing in my shoulder, and I never quite mastered meditating, but I just kept moving and eventually ended up where I was supposed to be. And at the very beginning, when I had no idea where I was going, at least I was moving away from the place I knew for sure I was not supposed to be.

Sometimes you need to do something, even if it's not neces-sarily going to end up being *your* thing. Move in a direction, any direction, even the wrong direction. Because rolling around in the rubble is not how we get better—we have to move.

A lot of my midlife crisis / New Me journey felt very "fake it 'til you make it" while I was undertaking whatever new hobby that came across my path. I knew I wasn't going to magically end up a runner, or a yogi, or a stoner (I do, however, have nat-ural munchy abilities that cannot be denied). But I also knew I wasn't a huge fan of who I'd become by the end of my marriage, and you may feel the same way.

It's okay if the moving doesn't feel natural at first and if it takes you quite a bit of faking it before you get anywhere near making it to the other side. Just don't quit. Just keep moving and punching and chi-ing. There is nothing in this world that is worth your effort more than making it to the version of yourself that is waiting beneath all that rubble of your divorce explosion.

You'll get there. I promise.

New You Checklist

If you are like me and need to crowdsource your personal growth, here are a few suggestions to maximize your impending midlife crisis. You do not need to do them all, obviously. Be really scientific about how you approach things, like I was. Close your eyes, put your finger on the book, and do that thing. Repeat until your chi is satisfied.

Move Your Body

Run

Walk

Hike

Yoga

Yin

Cycling

Weight lifting

Crossfit

Boxing

Swimming

Tennis

Cornhole (this is a sport, I promise)

_____

_____

_____

Move Your Mind

Meditation
Therapy
Reiki
Join a book club
Join a bunco group (this is a thing, I promise)
Join any other group that is an excuse to get together
    and drink wine and gossip
Join any other group that is an excuse to get together
    and drink tea and gossip
Weed
Cooking lessons
Read all the books
Listen to all the podcasts
Nap with intention
Learn a new language (if this seems a bit ambitious,
    maybe just watch a foreign film and call it growth)

_____

_____

_____

Maybe Don't Do These

Go skydiving
Get a tattoo
Buy a ridiculous car
Date younger people

_____

_____

_____

23

The Other Side

(and then, all of a sudden, it's behind you)

In the beginning of the 2020 pandemic, the world was on lock-down. It was an odd time to say the least. The kids were home twenty-four hours a day, Elizabeth and I were on the cusp of our divorce, and there was an egg shortage happening in the grocery stores. All these facts played heavily into me saying yes when our daughter asked for pet chickens. The kids were bored, I was moving out of the house soon (and would there-fore not have to deal with said chickens), and it's never a bad idea to have your own source of eggs during an impending apocalypse.

When our divorce was settled, and I moved back into our family home, I insisted that Elizabeth take the Cluck Cluck Bunch to her new house. She had always wanted chickens, and I was not interested in operating a farm in my backyard.

Unfortunately, all of my plans backfired about six months later when Elizabeth's new HOA gave her an eviction notice for the Cluck Cluck Bunch. I really, really didn't want to bring the hens back to my house, but the thought of letting them live somewhere else was breaking my daughter's heart. And so. The Cluck Cluck Bunch waddled back onto my property.

There was a lot of work that needed to be done to get my backyard chicken-ready once again, and Elizabeth agreed to help me with it, because she knew how important these chickens were to our daughter. I was skeptical that we could accomplish the tasks without incident, since we'd never been very good at collaboration when we were together. All previous attempts at team projects ended in a fight and an abandonment of any hope of cooperation.

When Elizabeth arrived at my house with the chicken coop, it had been about a year and a half since we broke up. It had not been the smoothest of eighteen months for the two of us. But somehow we'd gotten to the point where we were both willing to give this chicken project a shot. We had to build the coop and the kennel, as well as the fencing that outlined the designated chicken area in my backyard. The project took a couple of days. There was manual labor, power tools, instruction booklets, lunch breaks, and above all, collaboration.

The whole thing felt a bit like the "wax on, wax off" montage of *Karate Kid*. On the face of it, we appeared to be building a chicken habitat, but when examined closer, we were really working toward the other side of our relationship.

There were no arguments. Normally, I would get frustrated that she needed to be so collaborative, because I'm more of a divide and conquer sort of worker. But she said to me at the beginning, "I know you don't understand it, but I just work so much better when there is someone working with me. So, I need you to just be here and not go running off to do something else you think should be getting done." I listened and stayed near her the entire time, handing her nails and tools as needed.

Normally, she would barrel through the project, paying no mind to my input that I had gleaned from reading the actual instructions. But this time I could see her physically stopping herself from interrupting me or disregarding what I was saying. She'd listen to what I had to say, we would troubleshoot together, and we'd laugh it off if we hit hiccups along the way.

As we worked, we talked about everything under the sun. Our kids, her new relationship, this book, our families, and our failed partnership. Something about the long hours, manual labor, and lack of eye contact opened up these conversations to depths that we hadn't explored in years.

Following Day 1 of our project, after Elizabeth had gone home, I was flittering around my kitchen and saw a crumbled-up paper towel on the counter. I was triggered. I'd spent years cleaning up Elizabeth's messes, including her damn paper towels all over my kitchen.

The next day I pointed it out to her, annoyed, "You left a dirty paper towel on the counter, like you used to always do, and you just—"

"I know, I did it on purpose because it drives you crazy."

I laughed and shook my head. She cleaned up after herself throughout the rest of the project.

By the end of Day 2, when the chickens were clucking around their new home and our daughter was excitedly throwing them treats, it felt like something had shifted.

Elizabeth said, "We never could have done this project when we were together. What has changed?"

"Everything."

Everything has changed. The two of us have changed, our family dynamics have changed, the way we communicate with each other has changed, the grace we give each other has changed. Elizabeth wondered why we couldn't have gotten to all these changes when we were together. And we both agreed that just wasn't our story. We will raise these children together, and we are both committed to doing that project exceedingly well. That is our story.

It's not the story we had in our heads when we were young kids thinking about what our family would look like someday. It's not even the story we had in our heads decades later when our relationship was imploding. But it's what has been written for us, and for all of its painful plot points, this story has done a pretty good job finding its way to a happily ever after for all of us.

Our family looks and feels a little different now; there are two homes instead of one, life has expanded and contracted into different shapes, and our kids now have two happy parents. We always knew there was something better waiting for us on the other side of our broken union; it just took us a while to build up the courage to go looking for it. And then once we each found our peace independently, it took even more courage to reconnect with each other, to reach out from our new locations, past our history and hurt, and figure out a way to do this project together for our kids.

Everyone's timeline is different when it comes to post-divorce healing, and some couples never quite make it back to each other for the sake of the kids because their history and hurt is just too deep and wide to traverse. But if you are at the beginning of things, try to keep your mind open to a time when it may all be a little *less*. Less intensity, less anger, less hurt.

Don't beat yourself up if everything still feels like a lot right now and if the thought of less feels nearly impossible. Time is the only thing that can really get you from one side to the other, and the clock moves at different speeds for everyone.

And even if you never get to less with your ex, I promise you that eventually there will come a point when you have your chicken coop moment. When you look around at your life and yourself and you realize everything has changed. You are no longer in the raw phase of a life changing shape; you have become the new shape, and you are okay.

Keep your eyes on your reflection as the months and years pass, be sure to acknowledge your growth, however small, at every step. Keep moving, even if yours doesn't always seem to be the most linear of journeys. Then one day, without fanfare, and most likely without you even noticing, you'll be on the other side of all this.

I promise.

FUCK YOU, YOU FUCKING FUCK (A TIME FOR JOURNALING)
Time Capsule

For our final FYYFF journaling exercise we are officially done talking about the ex and are focusing solely on you.

But first, something about me.

Years and years ago I trained for a marathon. I am not a runner (see also my book *The Nonrunner's Marathon Guide for Women*). At the beginning of my training, after I stumbled through my first short run, I ended up face down on my kitchen floor, trying desperately to get my heart rate under control while also using the cool tile to bring my boiling body temperature down. I might have poured water straight on my head and tried to slurp it into my mouth as it fell to the floor. It was quite a display of athleticism.

My training was a fundraiser for the American Stroke Association, so to rally donations I would send out weekly updates detailing what happens when a couch potato decides to run 350 miles in four months. Spoiler alert: it was funny to everyone but my poor knee joints.

These weekly updates became a journal of sorts that forced me to document my pain and agony in real time. I wasn't looking back on the experience and recapping it as a whole; I was diving into the details of each week as they were occurring. In the end I had an amazingly thorough account that took me from my kitchen floor face-plant all the way to the finish line of a 26.2-mile race. I was brutally honest in these weekly recaps; some weeks I amazed myself at my progress, and other weeks I took naps on park benches at Mile 12.

The person I was on my kitchen floor was a completely different version of myself than who I became by the end of my marathon training. And lucky me, I have written proof of my transformation.

Healing from divorce is a marathon of sorts. It's long, it's painful, it involves random bursts of cussing and/or crying, and also the occasional carbo-load. But on the other side of all the hills and heartbreak is a completely different version of yourself waiting for you. And I don't want you to miss the opportunity to really appreciate how far you've gone on your route.

Whether or not you know it now, you are already well on your way to something so much better than your current mile marker. But the only way to truly appreciate how far you will travel is to check in on yourself periodically and really absorb the progress you are making.

Today your assignment is to answer my prompts below or to just randomly journal what you are feeling at this exact moment in time. Don't sugarcoat it, but also allow yourself to be bold in your ambitions for what Future You will be up to. And then check in every few months to let Past You know how far you have come and how much more you have left to accomplish.

Continue to do this throughout the next year or so. Even if you aren't feeling particularly accomplished, even if maybe you run into a stretch where you need to sleep on a park bench for a while (metaphorically, of course). That's okay, that's a leg of your journey, and all the different miles add up to where you are headed.

After a year (or two, or three), I hope you can look back on these journal entries and see your story written out in great detail for you. I hope you can see where you had the wind against your back and where you struggled with unexpected inclines. I hope you can see the value in all of it. And I hope you can carry it with you always as a reminder that you are a fucking champion.

TODAY: _____

Shit that is hard

_____

_____

_____

_____

Shit that I'm kicking ass at

_____

_____

_____

_____

Shit that is hard, but I've convinced everyone I'm kicking ass at

_____
_____
_____
_____

One goal I have for my next three months

_____
_____
_____
_____

How I've changed

_____
_____
_____
_____

One thing I want my past self to know

_____
_____
_____
_____

THREE MONTHS LATER: _____

Shit that is hard

_____
_____
_____
_____

Shit that I'm kicking ass at

_____

_____

_____

_____

Shit that is hard, but I've convinced everyone I'm kicking
ass at

_____

_____

_____

_____

One goal I have for my next three months

_____

_____

_____

_____

How I've changed

_____

_____

_____

_____

One thing I want my past self to know

_____

_____

_____

_____

Afterword

When I was a teenager, I spent my summers teaching swim lessons to little kids. Some of these children were TERRIFIED of the water. During the lessons all the kids would gather in the pool on these things called risers, essentially a fake floor, allowing them to touch in a part of the pool that was a couple of feet too deep for them. I would take the kids one at a time into the water to work on their lesson. The kids who were TERRIFIED would go into panic mode the second they were off the riser. They couldn't touch the bottom of the pool, and for all they knew we were in the ocean. Their body would tense and flail and fight, they would wrap their legs around my waist and dig their fingernails into my neck and arms—a death grip. It was all a natural human response to the feeling of impending demise, to the solid ground disappearing beneath them.

What these kids didn't understand was that being tensed up, the flailing, the fighting—all of that was what could actually cause them to drown. A tense, flailing body will go straight to the bottom of a pool. But if they would just relax, release the death grip, and be still . . . they could float.

My job over the course of the lessons was to get these kids to a point where they trusted me enough to release their grip, put their head back in the water, and unclench. I would always keep my hand under the back of their head; the point of connection

made them feel safe, even though in reality I wasn't actually helping them float; they were doing it all on their own.

I'd repeat, over and over, holding their eyes with mine, "You
can do it, all on your own, you *are* doing it." The look on their faces
was always the same, no matter the kid. A look of pure wonder, of
the whole world opening up because of what they found in themselves on the other side of their fear.

When we got to that point, when they were floating on their
own, when they trusted that they could float on their own, then
we could move on to actually learning how to swim. But first they
had to be still, they had to let go and believe that they would be
okay, even though every instinct was telling them the opposite. It
was like a trust fall, and it was a lot to ask of a little kid who felt
like they were in the middle of the ocean.

Divorce, or any life explosion, is a lot like learning how to
swim. It almost always results in the flailing, the panic, the grab-
bing onto anything and everything with a death grip, because we
are off our riser and have no idea how deep this new water is. It is
why people marry the first person they date after a divorce or grab
on WAY TOO TIGHT to that person. It's why they take on five
hundred different new hobbies or make ill-advised purchases or
go on crash diets. They are desperately grasping for a buoy; they
don't trust that they can float on their own.

I think the flailing of divorce has to happen, because the
flailing is the manifestation of the grief and the anger and the
breaking apart of lives and hearts. But I also think if we give
ourselves the chance to be still, to unclench, and to just release . . . we can and will float. We need to trust that we can
be okay just floating for a minute, on our own. We don't need a
buoy. Then, when we are ready, when we allow life to come to us
as it's going to come to us, for the water to ebb and flow as water
does . . . then we can learn a new way of swimming in this new
depth. But there can't be any swimming, any moving forward,
until we stop flailing.

It's worth noting that none of my scared swim lesson kids went from terrified to floating to swimming without setbacks along the way. Fear and flailing don't just disappear because of one successful fifteen-second float. The progression from hysteria to confident swimmer was never linear and always included periodic freak-outs, tensing up, and sinking. In those instances, I would pull the child to me, allow them to reengage the death grip, while reminding them what they already knew they were capable of. They'd wipe the water and snot from their face, take a deep breath, and unclench again. I'd hold their head in my hand again, providing the connection they needed to regain their confidence.

The "meantime" of divorce, the time between when you step off that riser and when you make it to the other side of the pool, is a different amount of time for everyone. And every journey will vary too, with stillness, flailing, and exhilaration all intertwined in your story of getting to the other side.

Wherever you are on your particular journey, I hope that you are able to give yourself grace. You don't know exactly where you are going or exactly when you will get there, but trust that you will find your way, even when every instinct is telling you the opposite.

Allow yourself to be still, exhale, and let life unfold. Feel free to use this book, or your friends, or your kids if you need a little point of contact on the more difficult days. And never stop trusting that there are so many great things waiting for you on just the other side of your heartbreak and fear.

You can do it, all on your own—you *are* doing it.

Acknowledgments

In looking back at this book and thinking about all the people who helped me get it to the finish line, I see that most of those people were the ones who were also there to help me through the meantime of my divorce. This book and my divorce were both huge emotional undertakings, and I'm still a little stunned by the amount of people who showed up to help me through both. I'm not the easiest person to help, and both of these experiences didn't exactly make me the funnest person to be around. But there they were. My people. Showing up. Over and over again.

The biggest thank-you for the existence of this book goes to my agent, Lilly Ghahremani. After more than fifteen years of working together, Lilly is now a friend as well as a professional ally. She pushed me to write this book well before I knew I had anything to say, well before I knew I really, really needed to write it.

Next up, Renee Sedliar took a chance on me, and on this book, and spent months using her editing prowess to wrangle me and my mess of emotions into something suitable for mass consumption. Believe me when I tell you that my emotions and I did not make Renee's job an easy one.

And then there was everyone else. All of my friends who had to listen to me process a divorce and a book deadline concurrently. My therapist, who worked double time to help me get into the right headspace for honesty. And my Divorce Squad, who spent hours upon hours sharing their hearts and deepest injuries with me, trusting me with both.

I'm not sure what I did to deserve all these people, but I do know there is no way that I would have survived the past few years without them. This book and my heart are so much better for having been protected, challenged, and embraced by all of you.

Thank you, thank you, thank you.